GET DIVORCED
BE
HAPPY

HELEN THORN

GET DIVORCED

BE

HAPPY

How becoming single turned out
to be my happily ever after

Vermilion
LONDON

1

Vermilion, an imprint of Ebury Publishing,
20 Vauxhall Bridge Road,
London SW1V 2SA

Vermilion is part of the Penguin Random House group
of companies whose addresses can be found at
global.penguinrandomhouse.com

First published by Vermilion in 2021

www.penguin.co.uk

A CIP catalogue record for this book is available from
the British Library

ISBN 9781785043697

Printed and bound in Great Britain by Clays Ltd, Elcograf S.p.A.

The authorised representative in the EEA is Penguin Random
House Ireland, Morrison Chambers, 32 Nassau Street, Dublin
D02 YH68.

Penguin Random House is committed to a
sustainable future for our business, our readers
and our planet. This book is made from Forest
Stewardship Council® certified paper.

For Matilda and Hugo, my brilliant children
and my everything.

And for Ellie Gibson, my comedy wife and best friend.

CONTENTS

INTRODUCTION

'Hey Helen, you're looking so
happy since your divorce. Should
I leave *my* husband?'

Since 'coming out' as single in 2020, I have received hundreds of messages from women around the world asking me whether they should leave their partners, how to know when it's the right time to go, or what online dating is *really* like. It has been incredibly heartening that people feel they can trust me with such big life decisions. But what can I reply to women I've never met, whose partners I don't know, whose relationships I've never witnessed?

Part of me just wants to say, 'Hi Susan, yup, definitely leave him, forge a new life, get a tattoo and discover the joys of fucking twenty-something men you meet on Tinder.' Because I truly think if they are asking a stranger on Instagram about their marriage, then they really already know the answer to these questions. They want out. They want better. They want to be happy. And the realisation that we don't have to be miserable or put up with shitty partners any more is a powerful shift for women everywhere. There is a deep rumbling in our culture; the tectonic plates are moving and creating a new landscape for us to be single, free and fabulous.

In the past few years, divorce rates have been increasingly rising and there has also been a significant drop in the number of both heterosexual and same-sex couples getting married. The pandemic has obviously contributed to this, as there's nothing like being locked up 24/7 with a partner to find out whether or not you really want to spend the rest of your life with them. But this is only part of it. Through strong voices on social media, a change in how we perceive single life and solo parenting, and the way in which we now champion our confidence, self-love and self-worth, we are gaining the strength to end or change relationships we would have previously endured. We stayed in crappy marriages because that is what society has always celebrated: couples are good; separation is bad. But, this, thank fuck, is changing.

In 2020, an article in *The Sunday Times* entitled 'The Power of Being Single', by journalist Fleur Britten, cited extensive academic research that suggests there is a new 'single-positive' trend emerging. And that prediction is 'that by 2030 single-person households will see faster growth than any other household type globally'. More and more of us are becoming single and are much happier for it. Us singletons aren't waiting to be fulfilled by a partner; we have everything we need. Britten, herself a single working mother of two, says, 'My headspace and my diary are at capacity, my heart and bed brimming.' Millennials and younger people are now actively choosing to live alone and 'won't settle for unhappiness' and, overall, we are starting to see the 'uncoupling of society'. I, like Britten, am thrilled to be part of a new trend of being very single and satisfied. And I won't stop spreading the word about it, either.

Across social media, there are thousands of accounts and individuals that are single and proud, and more and more women are championing the virtues and joy of living alone. This is starting to have a huge impact. Australian author and feminist Clementine Ford speaks and writes extensively about the power of women leaving toxic relationships. Clementine told me, 'I get so many messages on Instagram from women saying, "I have left my husband; it's the best thing I ever did, and I wouldn't have done it if I hadn't started following your posts. You gave me the courage to do it!".' She adds, 'Women just need to see that it is possible. It is not necessarily going to be easy, but we just need to know that it is possible.'

Sharing positive stories of separation and singledom is creating waves. I adore that women contact me and feel comfortable talking about their relationships, even if I am entirely unqualified to help them with their difficulties. It is true that I am gloriously happy that I became single in my early forties, and I do like to shout about it, a LOT. If I could be a superhero, I'd be the Divorcinator, setting women free from the clutches of shit marriages. SHAZAM!

But I want to be clear, I am *not* against marriage, love or romance, because when it's good, it's brilliant. I loved being in a couple and having someone to share my life with – well, most of the time. We had our ups and downs, and we went through couples counselling over the course of our relationship. But I simply didn't want to contemplate that there was even the slightest chance of getting separated. It was what happened to other people, not me. I believed wholeheartedly that my husband and I were going to be together, forever, right to the end, even when I would be wearing nappies and he would be on his second hip replacement. I was in love with being in love.

And then, on a cold night in March 2020, I suddenly became single. And when the world shut down a few weeks later, I found myself in a world of homeschooling, wine and cigarettes, with no friends to hug, no pubs to escape to, no overpriced spa days to soak away my misery. If Bear Grylls had designed divorce, this was it: extreme divorce in a global pandemic.

It's funny how little we prepare for something we have such a huge chance of encountering. With 42 per cent of marriages in the UK ending in divorce, it is extraordinary that we don't give it more thought when getting married. In all honesty, I think I spent more time making sure I had a fire blanket for the kitchen and an emergency breakdown kit for the car than I did contemplating that I, one day, would become a single woman again – even though the chances of this were far higher than my cooker going up in flames. In a world where you can't even get a takeaway cappuccino without a warning message on the cup, it made me wonder where the risk assessment forms are when you sign a marriage contract? Shouldn't wedding rings come with a safety warning? Side effects may include sudden heartbreak, loss of assets and having to decide who gets the cat.

Divorce and separation is a reality we don't want to think about when we are buying our bridal gowns, sorting seating plans and working out if we can afford to have Aunty Mary and all four cousins. Or, if you don't go down the marriage route, and are in the blissed-out 'setting up the forever home and happily-ever-after life together' stage, you don't want to pop that love bubble with thoughts of a messy end. Because it would be nice to think it won't happen to you, but chances are it might, and if it doesn't, it will happen to your neighbour, your best mate or your mum. Divorcees and singletons, you see, are everywhere. And guess what? This is a good thing. In ending a toxic relationship, or just parting ways when things aren't working any more, people may just eventually find unwedded bliss. Because, as I have learnt this past year, and many others have told me, separation is not a 'failure', and it is certainly not anything to feel shame about, or cover in secrecy. Becoming single is, for most people, an opportunity for happiness and, frankly, a better life. So, why, when it is so common, is it still such a shock and just so absolutely shit when it *actually* happens?

Little did I know that, over my first year of being single, I would face a bizarre series of events spanning from rock-bottom sadness, alcoholism and a broken eye to sexy underwear, online dating mishaps and an encounter with four hunky firemen. The whole thing was a shock, a hideous mess and then an absolutely glorious blessing. A year after ending a very long, sometimes wonderful, but sometimes very painful marriage, I am once more myself. And I realise I am much better off being a whole single person rather than half of a dysfunctional double. I feel like skipping down the aisles of ASDA and yelling, 'I AM SO FUCKING HAPPY!'

While it is undeniably sad and hard in the beginning, and involves a massive upheaval, the end result can give you unbridled joy. And the happiness on the day that the decree absolute comes through can equal that of any nuptial. So why is it that we only celebrate the beginning of a marriage when often it's the end of one that turns out to be 'happily ever after'? Where are the separation parties? The stack of 'Congratulations! The Arsehole's Gone!' cards, or the gift registry at John Lewis to buy gorgeous things to give to your newly single mate? Come on, it's 2021: it's time we looked at what it means to be single and celebrate the happiness of starting a new life, alone.

For me, it has truly felt like waking up in Oz: everything is in Technicolour; the witch (my marriage) is dead; people (my friends) are singing and dancing; and there are at least three men (on Tinder, Bumble and Hinge) accompanying me at all times – but more on that later in the book, she winks.

But to get to this point, my mental and physical health have taken a battering. It's like the first year of having a baby: I have had no sleep; I have lived off biscuits; there are many scars and stretch marks; and I feel completely different about my vagina. But I have come out the other side a better, stronger and happier woman. A woman I never knew I could be.

In the upcoming chapters, I will tell you about my experience of the first big year of separation, how a group of women held me together, and how lifting heavy weights got me out of the hellhole. Through the mess of it all, I have found confidence, desires and passions that I had hidden away for so long. With the help of experts, comedians and some other wise humans who have gone through it all, I want to encapsulate the comforting words that helped me recover while celebrating just how wonderful becoming divorced can be. And in finding out that one man didn't love me, I discovered that a whole army of women truly did.

This is very much my story and my perspective on the events that happened. I have changed names and kept individuals anonymous out of respect for their privacy. And their version and feelings will, of course, not be the same as mine. But I don't want to shy away from my own truth and journey of recovery. Every separation is different, and the way in which we deal with the trauma, grief and change isn't linear or predictable.

I couldn't have got to this point of joy and recovered so well, and frankly so quickly, without the incredible humans who came to my rescue. Friends, family and random strangers surrounded me with love, support and stories that guided me out of the darkest shit-pit and into the sunshine. I want this book to echo this and to feel like a thousand hugs and voices that can rescue and reassure you too.

While the end of your relationship may be the hardest thing you will ever have to face, you can do it, and you will survive and thrive.

1

Why I Loved Marriage so Much, and
Why I Was Afraid of Divorce

had always wanted a Vivienne Westwood dress, so I decided to make a trip to London from my home in Cambridge to find one to wear for my upcoming wedding. It was March 2009 and we were to get married at the beginning of 2010. My daughter was five months old at the time and I was breastfeeding her every three to four minutes. My body was still recovering from pregnancy and childbirth, and my boobs were like overstuffed water balloons. Time to try on some expensive clothes!

I went to a shop in Conduit Street and stripped down to my big pants and maternity bra. Then I tried on a fabulous cocktail dress made of raw silk. It had a bodice that nipped me in at the waist and gave me the most magnificent cleavage. The size 18 fitted well. And that was it. This was the dress.

I knew that a local boutique in Cambridge was selling the same dress, and I decided to buy it there, so I rang them in advance. They sounded excited that I wanted the Westwood dress for my wedding. But when I rocked up looking like all new mothers do, like I had been sleeping in a skip, they were less than welcoming. I put my card down and said, 'I'll take the size twelve, please.' That's right. I went in and asked for an £850 dress, three sizes too small. Both of the shop assistants looked at each other and were a little puzzled. Then one of them replied, 'You do know you can't return the dress if it gets damaged.'

'I *know*,' I replied firmly but politely, while my eyes said 'GIVE ME THE DAMN SIZE 12'. Then they quietly packed up the dress in tissue paper, because that's what posh people do with their clothes. And I got my very small wedding dress. Because there was no way I was going to be a fat bride. Brides aren't fat. I was going to have to shrink.

And that was that. Now, as crazy as it sounds, the first time I actually tried on the dress was only about twenty minutes before I walked down the aisle. I was so frazzled with sleep deprivation and wedding insanity that I thought I would just get thin through willpower and determination. And what a fairy tale it would be if I simply fitted perfectly into the dress on the day! I stopped eating and breastfed my daughter around the clock. She got bigger and I got smaller.

On my wedding day, in a hotel room near the church, my bridesmaid and my best buddy from school used elbows and knees to zip and hook me into the Westwood bodice. And there I was: a size 12 (just)! I popped into the car and drove around the corner to the church to get married as a small(ish) bride! SUCCESS. Time to move to London, buy a house, get a slow-cooker, have another baby and live happily ever after.

It horrifies me now to think of what I did to get into that dress. At the time, it seemed that this was somehow what I was meant to do – change myself so I could fit the image of a slim, demure bride, make myself pretty for other people, for him. Because the images that surrounded us then, and indeed still to a large extent continue to do so now, trumpet the message that fat is lazy, that fat isn't pretty, that fat is not good enough. On my wedding day, I was the thinnest I had ever been and probably ever will be. I feel ashamed now that I felt so good about this at the time.

As a person who has always been less-than-slim, curvy, big-boned, plus-size, or to put it another way, JUST FAT, finding self-confidence and body confidence has been challenging for most of my life. I am now a UK size 18 and feel incredibly sexy and fabulous, but this acceptance and love for my lumps and bumps didn't come easy. As a chubby child growing up among sport-obsessed and bikini-wearing Australians, I was teased for being fat, ugly and a bit weird. I had all the classic fat-kid experiences, like being picked last for a team in P.E. and not being asked to dance at parties, and I had all the usual insults hurled at me too: 'Who ate all the pies, Helen?' . . . that kind of thing. So witty.

Even my own brothers commented on my body and appearance. 'Hey, Helen, have you thought of losing weight? It would make you look really beautiful.' Oh wow, thanks bro . . . and no, that thought had never crossed my mind. Another zinger from a brother was, 'Oh God, Helen, I hope my daughters won't get your thighs.' Here's hoping they get your sensitivity and charm, I thought.

Now that I am a comedian, you would think my self-worth was pretty high, right? Why would I stand up in front of a big crowd of strangers in a tight gold catsuit and attempt to make them laugh if I didn't have a whole lotta self-belief and confidence? Of course, it's the opposite.

So many of us 'funny people' have been bullied as kids or have a deep need for love, attention and approval. My comedy partner Ellie always said to me, 'The first thing the audience wants to know when you step out on stage is what's wrong with you.' And as one of the things that I have felt is wrong with me is my size, I must confess some of the first jokes I tell to a new audience are those about my long breastfeeding breasts, my flabby tummy, or my massive post-home-birth fanny. Lolololololol. In my case, I feel like I have to make fun of myself before anyone else notices that I'm the 'wrong size' to be on the stage. Or to put it another way, say, 'Look, it's OK, I know I am fat. Let's all get that out of the way!' This is, of course, entirely my own hang-up, because one of the things our audience has said is that it's so nice to see someone who looks like me on the stage; that seeing a body like mine up there makes them feel represented.

I mention these stories as part of the broader context of why being in a couple meant so much to me. I have realised in retrospect that, at some level, I thought me getting married would be the magical thing that banished those comments, hurt and feelings of not being good enough. If one man could promise he would love me, and only me, for the rest of my life, then I would be protected from that negative crap forever. Abracadabra, begone fat-shaming! Who cared if a random man in a car yelled, 'Oi, fatso, hurry up!' (which he did), as I slowly ran past him? I could go home to my old hubster who thought I was everything, and he would make me better. Marriage was going to make the shit stuff of my past just melt away, right? Well, we all know the answer to this.

But, up until a year ago, marriage was my religion: I believed in it; I was devoted to it; I thought it made me whole. When I suddenly became single, I realised that I could not remember a time when I hadn't wanted to be hitched. From playing brides as a young girl, to fantasising about marrying Jason Donovan as a teenager, to spending my twenties on an insane mission to be proposed to, and then finally actually being married, I had spent an entire lifetime thinking I needed a man to feel complete. And that divorce was not an option. Of course, now I know that the thing I never wanted – being single, being divorced – is exactly what I ultimately needed. Yes, even at forty-one, with two kids, stretch marks, skin tags, and an ongoing battle with piles.

On the day we separated, the end of our marriage made no sense at all: this wasn't in the script. We had met at university, and we had done all the things that couples do in their twenties – we'd travelled, gone to music festivals, got terrible haircuts and spent lots of nights out at the pub with our friends. I also had a successful career working in art galleries, had won a few stand-up competitions and was briefly in a TV show. I made friends wherever I went. In short, I had a very good life I had created for myself.

But I was insanely focused on becoming a bride; I was OBSESSED, always wondering when my boyfriend would pop the question. Every fancy dinner we went on, or any time we had a weekend away, I would think, 'Oh this is it, he's going to surprise me,' only to be disappointed when we, I don't know, just enjoyed a really nice meal. Silly me. Most people spend this time of their lives having flings and literally fucking about. If you were that person, bloody well done you! Not me; not this romantic tragic. Instead, I did grown-up things like buy a house, talk about ten-year plans and visit Ikea on a Sunday. Just waiting and wanting to be a wife.

As psychotherapist Esther Perel explains in *Mating in Captivity*, 'Despite a 50 per cent divorce rate for first marriages and 65 per cent the second time around; despite the staggering frequency of affairs; despite the fact that monogamy is a ship sinking faster than anyone can bail it out, we continue to cling to the wreckage with absolute faith in its structural soundness.'

Yup, I clung on to monogamy and marriage like my life depended on it. Of course I knew deep down there was a chance of divorce, or of infidelity, or of it just not working out, but I wanted the fairy tale. I thought that marriage was everything.

We did eventually get engaged when I was twenty-nine, once we had moved to the UK and were living in Cambridge. It was all a bit of a shambles really. I was so determined to get hitched that I had a genius plan; I bought myself a ring. A £10 Top Shop cocktail ring. I gave it to him and said, 'I really want to get married, and when you're ready to ask me, you can use this!' I ACTUALLY DID THIS. Because obviously he would feel no pressure whatsoever and I'd be totally chilled waiting for him whip the ring out.

I sigh at my younger self, but, to be fair, the plan worked. He eventually presented the ring to me, and, on a holiday back in Australia, we announced to our families over a pad thai dinner that we were going to get married. Because nothing says romance like noodles and plastic table cloths. The same week, all loved up, I fell pregnant. Those two big buses – marriage and kids – had come at once!

The next nine months were some of my happiest times in our relationship. We grew closer doing all the clichéd things – reading baby books together, writing endless lists of names, sorting out the spare room and going to NCT classes. We lay in bed at night, feeling my daughter kick inside my belly, and we were filled with excitement. Now that I had a baby coming, the wedding felt less important. We were going to share this child and be parents for the rest of our lives! How wonderful, how perfect, I thought.

I gave birth to my daughter at home. There were candles, classical music and a massive inflatable pool in our tiny lounge. I don't want to show off, but I even delivered my placenta onto a plastic Tesco shopping bag for the midwife to take away. Glamorous. And then I became a breastfeeding, baby-slinging, nice-cardigan-wearing, organic-cotton-muslin-toting smug middle-class bore. I utterly adored it. She was a screamer, but I didn't care. I had my gorgeous baby girl, and I felt complete. But as the months of no sleeping wore on, cracks in my love-bubble began to show.

It was obvious that I would be the main caregiver: I was the one who got up in the night because I was breastfeeding. So I became the comforter and the one doing most of the harder parenting shit. I would also be the one to do all the nursery drop-offs and pick-ups, apparently because the nursery was nearer my work. And I would do most of the cooking, too, of course, because I was home more. I could hear my own mother's voice leaving my mouth – things like, 'Don't worry, let me do it!' or 'It's OK, I'll get up, you need your sleep.' If you're reading this and haven't had kids yet, DO NOT DO WHAT I DID. Try your best to make sure the workload is even.

The first year of motherhood was a hazy blur, as it is for most people. But, on top of this, I decided that we should go ahead and plan the wedding. We were going to have it back in Melbourne so that we could have friends and family there, and so that my dad, a vicar, could marry us.

How could I not want to believe in love? Love is the best. When it works and is healthy, it is a wonderful thing, and you feel great about yourself. And besides, girls from my and previous generations were taught from a very young age that we were not complete without a husband. That the ultimate prize was to be loved by a man.

I realise that I'm not the only person to seek value and validation in a partner. So I decided to seek the wisdom of Arabella Weir, the brilliant actor, author and comedian (most famous for creating the catchphrase, and bestselling novel of the same name: 'does my bum look big in this?'). She has also written and performed a solo show based on her experiences of being bullied for her weight and the value society places in women's bodies. Arabella said, 'I absolutely think being bullied about your weight and told you're not pretty enough when you're young affects how you think about marriage. When you're married, you've now got someone who has legally promised to love and like you whatever you look like. This person has signed the contract; therefore you can think, "I am OK now!" It is like the man has made a public declaration to not bully you, and to like you through thick and thin (hah!), in sickness and in health. For a lot of women, getting married feels like you have passed the test. So, of course, that is going to have that super extra appeal. It is going to make you think you will get the unconditional love that you seek.'

Thank God my own children are now shown positive images of both same-sex marriages and strong female characters. But I had very few role models to choose from outside of the coupled heterosexual narrative. As a child I couldn't escape the fantasy of brides and marriage, because I pretty much grew up in a church. That's right, the place where WEDDINGS HAPPEN. From birth until I was nine, my father was a vicar, and I lived in the vicarage, constantly surrounded by weddings and baptisms and the belief that a husband was for life, not just for Christmas. Then there's also the fact that – after their eyes met across a pulpit (she a choirgirl, he the handsome curate at her church) – my parents got married and are still together over fifty years later. I was doomed to be hopelessly devoted to the blessed nuptials.

Mum became the dutiful vicar's wife and was excellent at casseroles, tea mornings and being a mother – she had five children. The house was pristine, and every morning we would wake up to the table laid for breakfast with lacy doilies and toast racks. I AM NOT MAKING THIS UP. The house was always filled with parishioners and Bible-study groups and, of course, couples visiting Dad to 'prepare for marriage'.

The language my parents and their friends used about 'singles' or 'divorcees' was heavily loaded: 'Poor lonely Lorraine'; or 'It's so sad that Dorothy is all alone.' Always with a head tilt, and always with – I'm afraid to say – a touch of smugness.

I clearly remember them describing the breakdown of their male friend's marriage over tea and biscuits. 'Well, you know, Graham would still be happily married if the "feminists" hadn't got to his wife!' Those pesky feminists, what with their flat shoes, hairy armpits and wacky ideas of equality and belief in the rights of women. Damn you, feminists! Had my parents considered that perhaps Graham's wife wasn't happy? Maybe G-Dog was a complete knob. Who knows? Best to blame the evil feminists, though.

Despite my parents' disparaging comments about these champions of equality, I eventually became a loud and proud feminist myself, and everything I do now tells the outside world that I am a strong independent woman. I have chosen the male-dominated profession of comedy; I'm in a female double act called the Scummy Mummies with an incredibly strong woman called Ellie Gibson; I write about women, perform shows to women and have an award-winning podcast about motherhood that supports women. But, to be honest, I was pretty shit at feminism in my marriage. I somehow blocked out all those years reading Germaine Greer at university and listening to *Woman's Hour* when it came to my relationship with my husband. It took divorce for me to realise how different my expectations of equality were with him compared to with the other people in my life.

While, for me, the path to a traditional marriage seemed like the logical one, this of course isn't the case for everyone. Many have had negative experiences of other people's marriages, such as those of their parents or other family members. Marriage can symbolise entrapment and misery, and, for many, the thought of commitment to one person for life is a nightmare rather than a fairy tale.

Then there are the people who are simply not represented in the heteronormative 'girl meets boy and has 2.4 children' storyline. Rosie Wilby, the brilliant comedian and author of *The Breakup Monologues*, told me that, when she was growing up, she felt very removed from these pressures. 'Someone like me from the LGBTQI community has to some extent already moved away a bit from that mainstream media narrative of what a couple looks like. And what a couple should be. In some ways, you are slightly free of that baggage.' This didn't mean, of course, that she didn't want love or a long-term relationship, but that, because of her sexuality, those expectations weren't prescribed to her.

'Certainly for lesbians of my age, in our forties,' she says, 'we grew up thinking marriage and children were not an option. When I was a student, I went on a same-sex wedding demo and staged a same-sex wedding outside York Minster, thinking that in fact there was no way in our lifetime that men or women would be able to marry each other. So, I assumed my romantic life would be very different, and that the narrative of marriage and kids was simply not available to me. I already wanted to celebrate being free of that. I still feel very much outside of society. And I am very conscious that, when we talk about relationships and break-ups, we need to talk about them in an inclusive way.'

Speaking to Rosie and many other people as I have been writing this book has made me realise that I have lived for a long time under a very big heart-shaped rock. And I am glad to be coming out from under it, finally. I was so blinded by my quest to be half of a couple that I rarely contemplated that I could live a happy life any other way.

Esther Perel reflects on the pressures we place on coupledom: 'Today, we turn to one person to provide what an entire village once did: a sense of grounding, meaning, and continuity. At the same time, we expect our committed relationships to be romantic as well as emotionally and sexually fulfilling. Is it any wonder that so many relationships crumble under the weight of it all?' This was it. Society and the media had told me that I could get so much from that one person. I had looked to him to solve things in me and make the hurt of the past disappear. I had spent many years just looking in the wrong place for love and acceptance, when it was clearly already in me.

The concept that you could actually be fulfilled by or want to be with the same person for an entire lifetime seems incredibly outdated, considering just how bloody long we are all living these days. As Ellie's mum once said to me, 'Marriage was invented when everyone died at forty.' And there is more truth than humour to this. Considering that the average age for divorce among opposite-sex couples in 2018 was 46.9 years for men, and 44.5 years for women, maybe we should rejig marriage vows so that there is a get-out clause in your mid-forties. After all, we have plenty of performance reviews in our professional careers and everything we own has a limited guarantee. So why not apply this practically to our relationships? Should we not at least go for a yearly marriage or relationship MOT to make sure all the parts are in working order?

Or perhaps take on the Danish approach to marriage? Helen Russell, author of the bestselling book *The Year of Living Danishly* and *The Atlas of Happiness*, was told the approach in Denmark is 'Marry first for kids, and then for love'.

Helen explained, 'Denmark has one of the highest divorce rates in the world, but it also, I believe, has the highest rates of marriage. So my Danish neighbour used to say "We like getting married so much, we don't mind doing it more than once." So there is far less stigma to getting divorced here; it's kind of normalised, as in, *it's perfectly OK to leave a marriage if it's not making you happy*. Which is weird coming from the cultures that certainly I – and I'm guessing you as well in Australia and your family – come from and have grown up with.

'I think what's really interesting is that in the UK, it seems like people get divorced for *a really bad reason* like it's infidelity, or it's addiction, or it's abuse, and of course, yes, of course you should leave that sort of relationship, and even reading something like Glennon Doyle's amazing *Untamed*, she's leaving because she's fallen in love with someone else.

'But in Denmark people get divorced because they are no longer in love with their partner, or they're no longer happy with their partner; and that still feels like quite a radical thing, and something that we're still quite unused to, in other places in the world.' Time to book myself a mini-break to Copenhagen.

My previous approach to marriage and divorce, it appears, is rapidly becoming outdated. Was my unhealthy attachment to marriage really about being loved, or was it a fear of being alone? Deep down, was I scared that no one else would love me? Perhaps I wanted to leave, but didn't have the courage to do so? If I am honest with myself, I am pretty sure one of the reasons I blocked out the notion of divorce was because it just felt like too much work. I just couldn't be bothered with the whole shitty admin of separating, and the thought of having to start again looked so exhausting. We had been together for such a long time, all our friends were intertwined, our families hung out together in Australia, and everything just seemed, well, OK. We annoyed each other a lot, of course: I was too messy and put the heating up too high; he ate too fucking loudly and left nail clippings in little piles in the bathroom. You know, the usual crap. But this didn't seem uncommon among our married friends.

In fact, these little niggles fuelled many of the jokes Ellie and I would do in our live *Scummy Mummies* show. It was almost validating and reassuring when we would write material about the drudgery of long-term relationships and then in turn see other women laugh and nod along to it. That meant those feelings and experiences were normalised, and by sharing them I felt comforted that this is what married life was meant to be like.

The loneliness of separating after a long-term relationship is one of people's biggest fears, yet many 'attached' people are probably already experiencing it. As Arabella told me, 'There is no greater loneliness than being in the wrong relationship.

Being on your own and happy is a million times better than feeling alone with someone else.'

There were hundreds of nights when I was married where we would hardly touch each other, or even speak, after the kids went to bed. We were both tired and too busy escaping into our phones or just being in separate rooms because we wanted to watch different TV programmes. There was little connection, and everything just seemed so functional. We don't see these scenes in the Disney movies: a few years into the marriage and Prince Charming's in a grump because Cinderella doesn't like watching *Game of Thrones*; she's pissed off because he's left his diamond-encrusted shoes in the fucking lounge again.

Even though there were bucketloads of happiness with the kids, and things would seem to work when we were on holiday or had time with friends, there just wasn't the sizzle and excitement. I loved making an effort for anniversaries and birthdays, and always wanted a dinner out together, but I can't remember the last time he said I was beautiful or sexy, or I felt 'wanted'. But although I knew it wasn't great, I just thought that was it. This was marriage: kinda good, kinda shit, kinda just OK.

But it really wasn't OK.

2

The Decision. The End. The Beginning.

'*H*e's *done you a favour. You're not going to believe me right now, but this will be the best thing that has ever happened to you. He's set you free.*'

This is what my dear friend Nelly said to me at 3am, a week after my life as I knew it had exploded. I sobbed down the phone to her and tried to process what he had done. *He has set you free.* She was right. For so many years, I had held on to the relationship so tightly, trying so desperately hard to make it work, wanting to be married so deeply that I needed something as drastic and as colossally awful as this to break that grip. Let's be clear, finding out so suddenly that your marriage is over is bloody awful, and I wouldn't recommend going through this hell to anyone. I am also definitely not giving *him* any credit for the happiness I have found, or for this chance of a new life – fuck, no. But in that moment of discovery, I finally saw what an absolute shitshow everything was and had been for many years. It meant I could finally let go.

While the end of my marriage was something I didn't see coming, and things hadn't been perfect for a long time, I had thought there was enough to keep going, and that it wasn't all bad. It was hope, not necessarily happiness, that kept me positive, and I genuinely thought that 2020 was going to be our best year yet. I realise now that I had spent the majority of our relationship waiting for it to get better, to feel lighter, for it to finally get easier. Next year, I kept saying to myself, next year will be better, for sure. We had just got through those really challenging early years with the kids, when money was tight, when marriage was functional rather than just fun. So I hung on for the good times, for the pay-off. You would think after twenty-one years I would have realised that wasn't really going to happen, right? What I was really waiting for, of course, was for him to change.

Yet I started 2020 in a particularly smug state, full of unbridled hope and ridiculous plans. It was the start of a new decade, the beginning of a new era in my life as a forty-something woman, the year that everything would finally come together. Whatever that meant. Alongside the usual get fit, get thinner, and be 80 per cent vegan bullshit, I was doing all the middle-aged clichés – training for the London Marathon, planning a summer holiday in a part of Italy 'not many people knew about' and even considering whitening my teeth. Ugh.

And I loved my job. I mean, I REALLY loved my job. We had somehow amassed a (small) legion of loyal podcast and internet fans around the globe, and in 2019 Ellie and I had sold out our first *Scummy Mummies* run at the Edinburgh Fringe. We had toured the UK performing in gold catsuits to packed-out theatres and received standing ovations. Yes, I will take a bow, thank you. I was getting paid to be a sweary, boozy, slaggy forty-something, and, frankly, I was having the time of my life.

At home I had two gorgeous children who were eight and eleven and finally sleeping through the night and wiping their own arses. After years of feeling knackered and frazzled with my small humans, motherhood was just starting to feel slightly easier. And after spending a decade living in a wonky wooden house, we could finally afford to do up our little hippy dream home on a cul-de-sac that can only be described as London's answer to *Neighbours*. In fact, we were just days away from signing an enormous mortgage to renovate the house; the architectural plans had been finalised, and we were about to embark on a six-month building project. (Thank fuck that didn't happen in the end. I've watched enough episodes of *Grand Designs* to have known it was never a good idea.)

To top it all off, I had a husband who I thought I adored. We had started the year by celebrating our ten-year wedding anniversary and had spent a gorgeous night away together by the beach. It felt like we were connecting again. On the outside, all appeared to be right with my world. This year was playing out like the romantic comedy film I had always wanted my life to be. Move over Jennifer Aniston. But 2020, as everyone now knows, had plans of its very own.

Quite how dramatic these plans would be globally was yet to hit home. And first, 2020 would lob me my own personal bombshell. Out of respect for my children, I won't go into too much gory detail, but I discovered the truth of the state of my marriage in the middle of preparing my daughter's Dr Who World Book Day costume. I found a letter to my husband in the pocket of his jacket and let's just say, it wasn't from me.

I felt like I was going to throw up and faint all at once, but I had to pretend I was OK in front of my daughter.

'Mummy, what's wrong?'

'Oh, it's nothing, darling, don't worry!'

'That doesn't look like nothing!'

She was right; it wasn't nothing. It was everything. As if World Book Day wasn't bad enough, I had found out that my life wasn't what I thought it was.

In the blurry minutes after I made my discovery, as I stood in the bedroom with my daughter, I just kept thinking, 'I'm fine, I'm fine, I'm fine, I'm so totally fine, yeah, this is all going to be OK, I'm fine, I'm fine, I can do this! Breathe, Helen, just breathe.'

On some level, I realised, I had always feared this might happen, and here it was, unfolding in front of me. I remembered the month before, holding him in bed, cuddling up and saying, 'Ohhh, I never ever want to get divorced.' There had been a whole lot of friends who had separated recently, and the thought of the same thing happening to us scared me. Maybe I had said that because I meant it, because I loved him, or maybe I had said it to see how he would reply.

I talked to Anna Mathur, psychotherapist and bestselling author of *Mind Over Mother*, about this. Had I been seeking reassurance? She thought so. 'It shows that there was already fear there, because, beneath it all, you always feared that you weren't enough. And when you have low self-worth, or when you've grown up feeling always less than, you're naturally going to assume that you are the problem, that the other person is better than you and you need to earn your way to that love and affection and that security, and you tell yourself that if you're not feeling it, then you mustn't be doing it hard enough. There's that need to be constantly reassured. And you obviously felt he wasn't giving you the affirmation, the love

and security that you needed, and that, after all, was right.'
Anna was spot-on; I had been frightened it was going to end.

After what I had discovered, I began being super jolly with
the kids. I went into autopilot and got dinner ready like I
always did, speaking in an overly cheerful high-pitched voice.
I knew he would be home at any minute, and I needed to
make sure the children had no idea what was about to happen.
I gave them both a screen and biscuits after dinner to distract
them, and then I waited for him to walk through the door.

Just before he was due to come home, I texted my three
best Aussie mates on our WhatsApp group. These are the
women I went to university with, lived in a shared house with
and asked to be the godmothers of my children. They have
known me for over twenty years and been my rocks. I told
them what I had discovered:

> 'My heart is pounding and he's not home yet. Trying to
> be calm and happy for the kids. Feel so broken. What
> an idiot.'

My best friend Taryn instantly replied,

> 'Oh honey . . . Just breathe . . .'

Ceinwen sent the next message:

> 'Can't overstate your strength and amazingness.'

And then Shannon-Kate a few minutes later wrote,

> 'OK. I just saw this. We can hold you through this.

Now, straight to counselling, don't delay.'

And just like that I already had my three wise women there to hold me and keep me together, even though they were on the other side of the world. I texted them all back saying,

'Such a terrible shame, but I'll be OK.'

But was I going to be OK? I had no idea.

He came in from work the usual way, dumped his bag in the corridor and looked at me standing there.

'What's up?' he asked.

'Oh, nothing. Can you just come upstairs with me for a second?'

'Umm . . . sure,' he replied.

We walked into our bedroom, and he sat down on the bed and looked at me. I told him what I knew and that we were over.

It wasn't explosive, it wasn't dramatic, it was just done.

I am a natural overreactor and show-off, but strangely this didn't seem the time to do anything over-the-top. My body felt numb. I just needed to stay sane. I had to get the kids to bed, then there were dishes to clean and toys to tidy. The next few hours went past in a blur. I got the kids in their PJs and read them stories as a tsunami of adrenaline rushed through me. It's amazing how you just cope, as a parent, isn't it? You just do what you can to protect your children.

Once the kids went to bed, I was able to focus on that small matter of my life totally collapsing before me. We went downstairs and just talked and cried. I whispered and hissed endless questions at him. But none of the answers were comforting or made much sense. And the big thing that kept circling around my head was, 'BUT I AM A NICE PERSON. Why is this happening to ME?'

It is striking that at no point did I think about saving the marriage. Both of us, it seems, had in fact been set free by my discovery of his betrayal. It was over, and there was no way of ever going back. I felt strongly that I could not have done anything to stop this from happening. I had loved him, and I had worked hard in our marriage. I'd wanted the best for him. It felt very unfair.

Strangely, I don't regret at all being kind or trusting or loving towards him, because, hey, isn't that what you're meant to do when you're in a committed relationship? But it turns out marriage doesn't guarantee anything.

Dr Karen Gurney, leading clinical psychologist and psychosexologist, told me that this is common: 'It is something I see a lot in my work with couples. It is the security of marriage that is actually not there at all. It feels like it is there because you are married, but it isn't; it's all an illusion.'

This divide between what each partner finds acceptable within the relationship and also how and why they justify their own behaviour became very apparent to me. I kept thinking about just how many unanswered questions there were.

During one of our difficult conversations I said to him, 'So, I haven't been loved properly, I haven't experienced true love?' I'd sobbed, and out came a loud, low, primal moan. He offered a seemingly heartfelt apology. But that apology meant nothing to me. I had given him my whole heart, and he had smashed it.

I asked Anna Mathur about whether she sees this type of behaviour in the work she does as a psychotherapist.

She told me, 'I remember when I was working with some high-profile men, and I would say to them, "You want to

29

have your cake and eat it," and they'd say, "Yeah, I don't see why I can't, because I have it, already; I've got both." It's so destructive. There would have been empathy there once, when they were a child, then along the way it just gets lost, or rather it served them well not to have it, so they got rid of it, but then again it's still there, it's not really ever gone forever. And he'll never get what he needs either, because he goes around it the wrong way and denies so much of himself and other people, in order to try and get it, and that's not sustainable. That does not (in the end) make loving, healthy, enjoyable, sustainable relationships that stand the test of time.'

Speaking to Anna was reassuring, but I also felt incredibly sad that we had got to this point in life and it was all such a miserable mess.

I felt stupid that I didn't see this in him, or see it coming. We were still doing so many things together and working hard at just getting through life together.

Four days before shit hit the fan we had both run the London Half Marathon. Like every other forty-something we knew, we were both into exercise and trying to pretend the ageing process wasn't happening. He took his training very seriously and had all the gear, techniques and lingo. I had trained too, but I was more haphazard in my routine and was a slower runner. I am naturally built for comfort, not for speed, and it was enough for me that my body could just 'do' running. While he talked of splits and running cadence and timing his gels, I was focused on just getting over the line. We were in the same race, but our approach was vastly different, and we wanted different things from it. And on the day, he finished an hour ahead of me.

I think we can all see the metaphor here. The race, of course, was also the story of my marriage; we started from the same place, and we were technically in it together, but he sprinted out of sight and across the finish line while I was still enjoying the run with no idea where he was.

On the night I found out about the truth and confronted him, he stayed in the house. I didn't want the kids suspecting anything. So we just went to bed like we always did, him on his side, me on mine. He fell straight to sleep, and I stayed awake shaking, my head spinning, texting my Aussie mates, googling like crazy to find out more any information that would make this whole crazy thing make any sense. It was like trying to complete the world's shittest cryptic crossword. It felt like I was being slammed repeatedly against a wall. I don't think I slept at all. I just waited for the sun to rise so I could get the kids into their costumes and pretend everything was OK.

World Book Day happened like it always did. We took photos in front of the bookcase, and they looked so happy. They were happy. I sent the pics off to both sets of grandparents, just like normal. Nothing to see here! We are all ABSOLUTELY FINE! I walked them up to school and smiled manically at the other parents, then came home and stared blankly into the kitchen. What was I meant to do now? Everything looked the same around me, but everything was totally different. Deciding the marriage was over was the first of hundreds of massive and painful decisions that needed to be made.

How and why you decide to separate has a huge impact on the way you process the break. To wring a little more out of the race metaphor, one person is always going to be ahead of the other. Let's face it, it's pretty unlikely you'll both wake up one day and turn to each other in bed, saying: 'Jesus, I'm over it, are you?'; 'Yeah, let's not do this any more. Snap!' Regardless of how it ends, there's a huge mix of guilt, anger and a lot of sadness.

I spoke to the comedian Jessica Fostekew, about making the decision to leave her long-term relationship and what that experience was like for her. She said, 'It got to a point where I was increasingly unhappy and then when my son was about two or three that started ramping up, and it wasn't because he was doing anything wrong. I was just like, "What have I done, what am I doing here, in this situation?" Not just in my beliefs . . . I think for years, really, everything that friends had said and therapists had said you could do to improve your relationship, you could be more tactile, don't just be like friends, even if it's just cuddling while you watch the telly, you know, I just found impossible to do. I just was like, "Why am I forcing this?" And then I thought things like – we'll go on holiday together, spend time together just the two of us, get away from our kid, maybe have a weekend in a hotel – and we did all those things, but that was when we would get on the worst!'

I asked her, 'So when was the moment you realised you had to go, that it was over?'

'We started looking at somewhere bigger to rent,' Jessica told me, 'and we found somewhere, where I live now, and we got it all sorted and everything. Then the day we signed the contract, I felt an absolute insurmountable wall of "you can't leave him", like this was an impossible thing to do, and suddenly I knew I had to get out because I was hurting everyone and going to destroy myself, and what is the point of being with him if I felt this disconnected. And I think emotionally and psychologically at that point I realised I'd been single for years. I mean, we'd been OK friends, we had been and still are, we're a good team at being parents; that's it. And he will hate me if he ever hears this, or reads this, but I think we're better friends now than we have been for years.'

In the early days of separation, I envied friends like Jessica who had just sat down at the table and talked it through. While incredibly sad, that at least felt fair, and a 'good' way to separate. But is there such a thing as a good separation? Can we avoid any of this initial pain? And how do we know when a relationship is unfixable?

After I'd had more time to process the initial shock of the separation, I spoke to Dee Holmes at Relate, an organisation that provides relationship support. Dee is a senior practice consultant and has years of experience helping couples. I wanted to know if there was a right way to end a relationship.

'It's a really hard thing to do. I think that's why people do things like have an affair, to step out and away, even if the other person doesn't know at that stage. I think also, ironically, the person who's having the affair or wants to go can often be quite cruel to the other person, picking fights and accusing their partner of the very things that they're doing themselves, and that's likely about not wanting to own their own actions and transferring it all onto the other person instead. It's not usually done maliciously or nastily – it's almost that the person doesn't like themselves for what they're doing, so they're pushing that out there.

'Often a trial separation or a decision to "have some time apart" can be tricky to read. I think there can be a lot of ambivalence for people, but I also think many people know exactly what a trial separation will lead to – they're just ending the relationship in increments. And when people say they want to leave with a "No, there isn't anyone else, I just want to be on my own; it's all about me, it's not about you," that can be quite cruel too, because for some people not having a reason can be worse than actually having a concrete reason like, "OK, my partner's met someone twenty years younger." Because then at least you've got a focus for your anger. I think that probably the best thing to do is for people to talk openly when a relationship starts to go wrong. People do fall out of love, but sometimes they don't realise a relationship has gone wrong until they're at a stage where they're not happy.'

'So how do you know if your marriage is over and it's time to separate?' I asked her.

'Relationships go up and down,' she told me, 'and they get good again, and they get bad again, and I think, for me, one of the key indicators that it may be really over is when the arguments stop being about things like who didn't put the rubbish out or what colour car to buy and instead become character assassinations of the other person – you know, "You always do this, or you always do that." As you know, your own children can become a source of argument in that you might parent differently to your partner. Arguments like, "don't be so hard on the kids, they don't have to finish their dinner," or "they should be in bed by now" are common, but sometimes they become bigger than the thing they seem to be about.

'Another sign is a lack of respect, because when you start to attack a partner's core, or their being, or everything about them, then you don't have any respect left. With couples I've seen as a counsellor, if I feel like they don't really respect each other any more, or if one of them doesn't respect the other, I get a sense of hopelessness, a feeling that maybe this relationship really has come to its end.'

Even though the end was a surprise, there were many points during our marriage when I thought my husband seemed withdrawn, and often, if I was downstairs in the house, he was upstairs, or if I went upstairs, he'd come downstairs, as if there was a physical as well as emotional distance between us. I knew at some level that something wasn't right, but I hadn't probed further. I wanted the marriage, and I wanted to be the mum and the wife and hold on to the family.

I shared these thoughts with Dee.

'Especially for women,' she said, 'I think keeping the family unit together is such a driving force, and I think that's why quite often marriages limp on until the very end. And I don't think that's good. I mean, obviously you ultimately want your children to grow up in a healthy, happy family, but if you can't have that, then it's best they grow up with two healthy happy parents who aren't together.

'But in order to separate fully, people need to have a bit of a split, and a bit of anger. With people that begin with an amicable separation, there's going to be a point at which the explosion will happen. They might start off nicely, and it might be fine. They split the house, and the kids go here or there, and then there might be something that triggers it going wrong – a not agreeing on how to separate shared possessions, or money, for instance. The other common trigger is when someone starts a new relationship. Often then, people who have had quite an amicable break-up until that point are like, "No, you're not taking the kids on a two-week holiday with your new partner," and that response can often take people by surprise. Having anger at the beginning, like you did, actually allows you to separate more fully, because your anger cuts the ties. Then, at some point, you are able to be more amicable around the children going forward.

'I think there has to be a period of anger to fully end one relationship and then come back into the new separated-parent arrangement. Of course, if you haven't got children it doesn't matter so much, as most likely you never have to see each other again.'

Dee is right. That anger did feel like a guillotine severing our partnership, very swiftly and very neatly. Separation involved dealing with a *lot* of anger, and I sat with it very uncomfortably. As a comedian, I am fairly positive, and I love to make people laugh; my whole being is about being fun and light. So those early days were really heavy and difficult. The hardest thing for me to get my head around was the fact that everyone else around me seemed to love me, but the person I was married to, whom I wanted more than anyone else to love me, simply didn't.

'What attracts people to each other is also the thing that repels people at some point,' Dee told me. 'This is just a hypothesis, but if your husband had periods of darkness, then your humour and lightness may have been what attracted him to you; but then of course it may be that thing, as time went on, that made him feel worse about himself in some ways. And that's not your fault, you know, you hadn't changed, but suddenly his experience of you, instead of it cheering him up and making him feel better, made him feel worse.'

Dee's speculation on this took me right back to when we had gone through couples therapy in our mid-twenties. Thinking about it now, who does that as a young person? Don't unmarried people in their twenties just split up if things are tricky enough to need therapy? I had obviously watched far too many Woody Allen movies about neuroses and anxiety and felt we too needed a shrink. It was during a time when my comedy career had just taken off in Melbourne. I had been in a TV show and won a couple of competitions, and I was on the brink of making it. My light was probably annoyingly bright by then. So let's move to a different country on the other side of the world. A fresh start? A new beginning? Maybe my light would look different over there.

In 2006, I gave up friends, my comedy career, my beloved job at an art gallery, and followed him to the UK. This was my choice. He never once told me to give up comedy or pressured me to move with him. But I was twenty-six, wanted kids soon, was desperate for his love and had convinced myself that this is what I needed to do. Because maybe, just maybe, we would be happier somewhere else, even though we were still the same people. He took a new job, an exciting one, in Cambridge. A job that made everyone go, 'Oh, that's so interesting!' and he seemed happier.

I couldn't find work in my field, so I got a lower paid admin job, and I decided to give up stand-up comedy, because it was all a bit hard, and I thought that I should just concentrate on us being happier together. Yup, I gave up something I was good at, that made me feel alive and fulfilled me in the most glorious ways. But it was all about give and take, wasn't it? This was *his* time to shine, right? And I convinced myself I didn't need to pursue the career I loved because it was time to simplify life. Just like Felicity Kendal in *The Good Life*. We went to farmers' markets on the weekends. We read the *Guardian* over coffee and croissants on a Saturday morning. We went on bike rides, we bought Delia Smith cookbooks and cuddled up on the sofa feeling content. Bliss. 'Come on, Helen,' I thought, 'you're nearly there! This is the final sprint! You'll be married soon.'

I had all but given up hope of ever doing another stand-up gig when late one night in 2013, as I was breastfeeding my youngest child, I had a life-changing moment. I just thought, 'Where the hell have I gone? What is it that makes me happy? When did I last feel amazing?' And I knew the answer. It was doing stand-up comedy. It gave me joy and purpose. I ached for it. The next day, I booked myself a crappy little five-minute gig at a venue down the road. A few weeks later, I stood up on stage under the lights. Another comedian saw me shine, but she didn't feel overshadowed; she felt illuminated. That person was Ellie Gibson.

Fast forward a couple of years, and Ellie and I had formed the Scummy Mummies and were on our way to success. The podcast had received wide praise, and we were performing to bigger and bigger audiences around the country. And, coincidently, this is when my marriage started to go into decline again. We went back to couples counselling. I remember our therapist saying, 'You have two choices: stay together or separate, but both paths will be hard.' Of course I wanted to stay married! I wasn't there for that other option. So we began eighteen months of soul-searching sessions. This time, though, I didn't end my comedy career, and I felt like we were getting closer and happier. He had suddenly found his exercise mojo too and started to lose weight. He looked great! But, unbeknownst to me, as well as starting a new life of fitness and excessive Lycra, he had also begun to leave me.

When I found out it was over and had been for some time, all my memories over the past years began to crumble. It was as if someone had gone through all our happy photos and attacked them with a machete. Holidays, birthdays, dinners out, trips to the park. I waded through this quagmire of shitty thoughts again and again. And cried. I did so much crying.

I realise now that I was in deep grief. So much of the life I knew had gone. I spoke with the author Alexandra Heminsley, who wrote a beautiful book, called *Some Body to Love: A Family Story*, about the end of her marriage. Her then-husband, just months after their son was born, told her that she needed to transition, and Alexandra decided that she would end the marriage. She explained, 'When you break up you're not just grieving for the relationship, but the rest of the relationship you were yet to have. And I felt that with D: we are still going to have a relationship, but it is just not marriage ... There is something that is really powerful in making something good from something that other people thought was broken. But, the marriage still had to be grieved for – and I won't shy away from that word, it is not like D died, but my marriage did. Grief doesn't have to be a death.'

One night, after we had put the kids to bed, and about a week after the decision to separate, we were having a particularly difficult conversation about what he had done. I went into a fiery rage, and couldn't contain my hurt and anger any more. My whole world had exploded and I felt out of control. What the fucking hell was happening to me?

BUT a separation is like a bear hunt: you can't go over it; you can't go under it; you've just got to go through it. Plough through the shit. Shout, get angry, cry and then cry some more.

The week after there was lots of information buzzing around in the news about the coronavirus that was happening in China. On the 8th of March, I got asked to go on Colin Murray's radio programme on BBC 5 Live. It was a late-night chat show and I thought, fuck it, I might feel insane, but at least it will get me out of the house. Away from any reminders of him.

I was on the show with another comedian, and we had to make funny comments about news items and issues. I do clearly remember the death toll in the UK was just five people AT THAT POINT and I felt pretty relaxed about it, like it wasn't a big deal and it couldn't possibly happen to us. Surely not here? I also remember us talking about the topic of finding humour in dark times – I know, the irony. I decided to recount the story about my granny's funeral. I confidently told a live audience across the nation that my four male cousins had been the pall-bearers and that two were really tall and two were much shorter. And when they carried the coffin, the tall ones were at the back, therefore creating a significant slope. When they lifted her up, we heard the matriarch of the family slowly slide down inside the coffin and bang her head as we walked her out of the church. LOL. And then I finished the anecdote with a loud, 'OMG, it was FUCKING hilarious!'

Cue me gasping then immediately covering my mouth! WHY DID I SAY THAT? Oh no, oh no, oh no, oh no, OH NOOOOO! … I JUST SWORE ON THE BBC TELLING A TERRIBLE STORY ABOUT MY DEAD GRANDMOTHER!

Colin Murray's face went pale; he apologised to the listeners and went to a track. I felt awful. Oh Helen, your marriage is in the toilet, you haven't slept in nearly a week, and now you've just ruined your career by saying the second-worst swear live on the BBC! Colin was lovely and he could see I was horrified about my potty mouth. He gave me a big smile and the thumbs up and reassured me. But I felt like I was coming down from drugs.

It's time to stop going into overdrive and battling through, Helen, I told myself. You need to stop pretending everything is OK.

I was spiralling down fast, and nothing could stop the racing thoughts and panic. I spent endless hours on the phone to my incredible big sister Claire, sobbing and just wanting her with me. She gave me all the time to cry, and space to try to understand all this insanity that was swirling around me. I tried to articulate what I was feeling, but I couldn't – I didn't have the words for this new and confusing pain.

As the blurry days of shock continued, it was clear we couldn't carry on with him staying at a hotel and coming in and out of the house. It was painful, and every time he was in the house, I felt uneasy and unstable. While I knew he was still great with the kids, I needed to be very far away from him.

I asked Laura Naser, a leading family lawyer and author, what her advice was for these early days of separation.

'The first thing is telling your partner that that's it,' Laura said, 'because communication is the first key thing – but doing it calmly, trying to be as Gwyneth Paltrow as you can, in terms of being amicable. One of the things that often comes up with my clients is that one person has made the decision and they've told the other person, but the other person is ten steps behind, because this is news to them – they're mentally not on the same page yet. So the communication of it is really important in setting the foundation of how the future communications are going to go – you know if you've shouted in an argument, if you've yelled, "We're over and I'm not going to pay the mortgage any more," all that can be really inflammatory, can cause panic and you're immediately at war with each other and you've lost trust. Then you don't know how you're going to pay the bills, you have to now ask (that partner/ex) if you want to use the car, for example, and it's suddenly all become really contentious, so communication is everything here. Be clear about the decision you've come to and make sure you give each other some time and space to come to terms with that.

'Then it's the practical stuff, so you are then looking at the immediate set-up, you know, like who's going to carrying on paying what? What are we going to do, where are we going to live? How are we going to tell the kids – what are we doing with the kids? All that immediate practical stuff. So, emotionally, you're going to both have to have that chat, and then you will need to move to who is going to live where? In lockdown, of course, this has been different, but usually for the majority of people, because of financial restrictions, it's not always available for people to immediately separate, go and rent somewhere else or buy another property, so you have to both live in the same house or flat for a bit. I'll go and sleep in this room, then you pick up the kids on these days, and I'll do their dinner and bath time and leave you alone, then on these days you do it and I'll leave you alone etc.'

So, it was time to get practical, and lockdown in the UK was imminent. He had to find a new place to live, and fast. There was no way I was going to spend months homeschooling, working and living in the same house with this man. He said he would consider living in a tent in the front garden, and that's when I had to find the strength to say what I wanted. I told him he needed a place nearby so the kids could go to school and they had a proper place to visit. The kids loved him, and he loved them back. A terrible husband, yes, but a very loved dad. While we didn't have a lot of money, we had enough for him to rent a small flat. I know this option isn't available to everyone. Some very close friends have had to live with their ex-husbands for months and sometimes years. It works financially, but the emotional toll is incredibly hard.

After a lot of back and forth, he managed to get a two-bedroom flat just a few streets away. It was perfect. I texted Ellie to tell her it had been sorted and that I could feel happy and have some sort of peace now. She asked me where the flat was, and I told her the street. She replied,

'No way, what number?'

When I told her, she typed back:

'FUCK OFF! FUCK THE FUCK OFF. THAT IS MY OLD FLAT. Me and Pete got back together in that flat.'

My soon to be ex-husband was moving into the place my comedy wife had reconnected with her husband. You could not make this shit up.

He moved out properly soon after. I had packed up all his clothes and things from the bedroom and put them into suitcases. I had removed all photos of him from around the house, taken out his books from the shelves and moved other painful mementos into boxes. I was still living in the house we had lived in for ten years, and our children were still half of him. He would be part of me, forever. I really do envy those who split with their partners without kids in the mix. I realised I would probably have to see him regularly for at least the next decade. FAAARCCKKKK!

I watched him packing things into the car. It was weird and silent. When the last box and suitcase were packed, it was time for him to go. Standing in the kitchen, I felt compelled to have one last hug with him. I was already starting to feel the absence of touch. When you're in shock and in the beginnings of grief, what you crave, even more than reasonably priced red wine and Marlboro Lights, is a proper boob-smashing hug. Little did I know this would be my last hug from an adult for the next three months. So I held him and then I quietly told him, 'It's time for you to go. This isn't your house any more.'

He looked hurt; maybe it was a cruel thing to have said, maybe I wanted to hurt him. I felt I was allowed to, and fuck, he had hurt me. But it was just the truth. This was going to be my house with the kids, now. And we had to start making a new life as a family of three. He said goodbye to the children, and then he drove away. And that was it.

It was the first day of lockdown and the beginning of my new life.

Things I have learnt about relationships and the shock of separation

- Don't be afraid to talk about hard and confronting things when you're in a relationship, because they will eventually come up and out when you are least expecting them. I wish I had asked more questions and probed a little deeper, and really talked about the fears I had.

- Seek couples counselling if there are things that you find difficult to talk about or need guidance as to whether you want to continue or separate. Having a calm and neutral space is important. It is 100 times easier to confront the shit stuff in the safety of the therapist's chair.

- There is no correct way to react to situations, but try to remain as civil as you can. Being angry is completely normal and understandable, but you might continue having a relationship with your ex if children are involved, so try to keep calm when you can. Use your friends to really let off steam and release all the big swears on them.

- Seek help from trusted friends and family immediately. And don't hold back the tears. Crying is important and healthy.

- Even if you split amicably, you are allowed to feel sad and also ask for help. The end of a relationship is really fucking hard, no matter how it ends.

3

The Messy Months: Discovering the Power of Anger, Sadness and 24-hour Clothes

How was I meant to teach long division *and* think about the horrors of my marriage breakdown? The world had shut down, I could only leave my house for one hour a day and I had to homeschool two children, all while working through the trauma of the separation and the end of my marriage. Come the fuck on, universe. I'm good at multitasking, but not *that* good.

You don't hear male soldiers or athletes saying, 'I don't know how I managed to survive in Afghanistan' or 'How on earth did I run a marathon in two hours?', do you? Nope. We hear (in detail) the training, the hardship, the 'journey' they undertook to survive. But if anyone knows about survival, it is women. Now is the point where I am tempted to write, 'I don't know how I got through the first months after the separation.' You know, the way mothers (me included) say things like, 'I don't know how I got through childbirth' or 'I don't know how I got through those first years of motherhood.' But now I have lived through another full-on life event, I am sorry to say this, but it's bullshit. You DO know how you got through the tough times. You worked bloody hard. You got up every day no matter how crap you felt and you got stuff done. Sure, some days you didn't get out of your PJs and you survived only on toast crusts and Jaffa Cakes. And yes, perhaps other days your only achievements were doing a poo and ordering a takeaway pizza. But you kept going. Because you're always stronger than you think you are. When a woman says, 'I don't know how I got through that!', she dismisses her struggle. And this plays into the patriarchy's hands, because it doesn't acknowledge how badass we are. So please vow to never say it again, OK?

Many things got me through the fug immediately after the separation: talking to friends and family endlessly; getting a good therapist; eating ALL THE CARBS; Deliveroo-ing myself everything from milkshakes and Dairy Milk to a ten-pack of cider; drinking and smoking whatever and whenever I wanted on my days alone; and working with Ellie on the Scummy Mummies. But sitting down with my feelings was the hardest and best thing that I could have done. Day after day, I was stuck in the family home, staring at the kitchen table we had sat around for ten years, at the pictures on the walls, the furniture, the towels we were given for our wedding; everything had been part of that previous life.

I devoured podcasts, books and anything on the internet that touched on what I was going through. Amy Poehler's autobiography *Yes Please* was particularly helpful and comforting. Her depiction of her comedy partnership with Tina Fey felt familiar and warm. Being in a double act is like a marriage, but far better. Sure, there's obviously less sex, but there are a lot more laughs. And the way she described what it feels like to have an audience laugh at your jokes was reaffirming. At times, I was feeling about as funny as a funeral, and to be reminded of the job I loved was a good kick up the arse. Her take on divorce is one of the most accurate I have read, too. 'Imagine spreading everything you care about on a blanket and then tossing the whole thing up in the air,' she writes. 'The process of divorce is about loading that blanket, throwing it up, watching it all spin, and worrying what stuff will break when it lands.'

When I was in the depths of separation and processing the grief, there were often times when I wanted to hide away from my feelings, from life and from my loved ones. As I had always been the self-appointed 'fun friend' to everyone, I didn't want to be the fucking joy vacuum of the group. I just wanted all the sad shit over and done with as quickly as possible, thank you, and back to nights of Prosecco and gossiping. But until then, sometimes I just needed to be under a duvet and spend three days on the sofa in the same joggers. I didn't want people seeing me in this state, and I hated that I couldn't give friends anything in return apart from tears and a crumpled body that smelled of fag-ash and Wotsits. But, as much as I wanted to push on without any help, I had to accept that I needed a huge gang around me to slowly pull me out of the trenches.

As the psychotherapist Philippa Perry wisely told me, the 'number one rule for getting divorced (or separated) is make sure you've got some mates. You want your gay mate, you want your raucous mate, you want your quiet listening mate, and the practical one. You need the whole shebang.'

I know everyone will cope with this experience differently, but believe me when I tell you this. YOU CANNOT GET

THROUGH THIS ALONE! It doesn't matter if you have kids, or are young and childless or if the relationship only lasted three years; it is a tough thing to conquer by yourself. You will need good buddies to help you navigate the rocky seas, bring you biscuits and wine and shout, 'This fucking sucks, mate!' This is not the time to be brave, stoic and bloody British about it.

So I accepted help from friends. People left lasagnes and bottles of wine. One day during lockdown, my friend Kim placed a packet of fags and an Easter egg on my doorstep and air-hugged me from two metres away. Never underestimate how much better these tiny gestures and interventions of love will make you feel. I know it is so difficult for many of us to accept support when we have always been the carers, but just take all those lasagnes, OK?

In these messy months or years (however long it takes), it is all about putting one foot in front of the other. Arabella Weir said: 'For the first year, just do exactly what you feel like doing in the moment. Do not put any expectations or benchmarks on yourself. Expectations are what make you depressed! Forget the word "should". You will get through the days, you will feed your children. Some days you'll feel great and some days you'll feel crap. It might take you six years to recover from the divorce and that's fine. But you will get there. Just focus on what you can do on a daily basis.'

These words felt like a hug. There were moments where I felt guilty about the state of the house, how little my children were learning and how we had all forgotten what a carrot looked like, but I realised this time wasn't going to last forever. And that it was more important that we had fun choosing a different movie every night and perfected the art of cooking microwave popcorn, and that we all felt loved.

Even though Ellie and I had to cancel our big tour of the UK, we still wanted to keep performing and creating comedy during the lockdown. Although I did announce my separation publicly a few months down the line, in the early days I just wanted to be private and come to terms with it myself. It was strange. I had spent nearly seven years talking honestly and openly about my experience as a mum and as a woman heading into my forties. Now I had to keep so much back about what was really going on, but all the while be AUTHENTICALLY FUNNY! It felt a bit like those first three months of pregnancy, when you're not supposed to tell anyone. Ironically the time when, in fact, you feel the worst and want the most sympathy.

Psychologist Dr Rachel Master told me, 'In the first year of separation, you're essentially in survival mode. Your brain is not functioning as it should. You're functioning for your kids, and trying not to have a mental breakdown. There is also an element of pushing away the sadness. You try to fill up all the space.'

Continuing our work was part of our survival as a duo, but it also kept us sane. And by all accounts it was needed by the women and mothers who followed us. So we began to do live shows twice a week on Instagram, as well as recording short comedy songs. We wrote sketches, played stupid games and sang songs about Covid and homeschooling. I hid the fact that I was doing this alone as a single parent, but frankly everything else was pretty much on display. I remember one morning, while the kids were downstairs consuming their second packet of Hobnobs for breakfast and the entirety of YouTube, I was upstairs filming myself dressed in a catsuit that looked like a big pink hairy vulva, singing the lyrics 'Gotta wider vagina, and I piss like a horse' to the tune of 'Eye of the Tiger'. Why we don't have our own Radio 4 show is beyond me.

Ellie was amazing; a powerhouse, a comedy machine. She took command and kept us going. In early April, I listened to an episode of the podcast *Unlocking Us with Brené Brown*, in which the American professor and podcaster explains that during anxious times we either behave in two ways: we either overfunction or underfunction. 'Overfunctioners tend to move quickly to give advice, rescue, take over, micromanage, get in other people's business rather than looking inward. Underfunctioners tend to get less competent under stress. They invite others to take over and often become the focus of family gossip, concern, worry. They can get labelled as irresponsible, or the fragile ones, the ones who can't take the pressure.'[1] You can guess which role Ellie and I each took.

That's right, I was definitely underfunctioning; but, strangely, this was the best thing I could do. Just stopping. Just allowing myself to live from one takeaway kebab to another secret Marlboro in the backyard, to yet another episode of *Modern Family*. But at the same time, I was also being an OK mum; no, damn it, I was being a great mum. I look back on a lot of that time with fondness. Our daily routine was to wake up and cuddle together, have some breakfast, watch screens, eat some more, go for a walk and then eat pizza and watch a movie. We basically repeated that daily for six months.

1 Brown, B. (2020). 'Brené on Anxiety, Calm + Over/Under-Functioning'. [Podcast episode]. *Unlocking Us with Brené Brown*. Available at: https://brenebrown.com/podcast/brene-on-anxiety-calm-over-under-functioning

The cuddles in the morning were my favourite. Each night, the kids would take it in turns to sleep next to me. I can't imagine what it was like for them suddenly having to deal with the separation, not going to school and being away from all their mates. I decided early on that their mental health was my number-one priority. Seriously, fuck homeschooling. So I tried to make home as fun and relaxed as possible. We ate beige food most nights, were covered in crumbs half the time and were probably on the cusp of scurvy. Brushing teeth was optional, as were baths, but we laughed and hugged and comforted each other. We held each other's (sticky) hands as much as we could and formed a new family of three. In short, we were a bit stinky, but a lot happy.

One of the things that brought us daily joy was a walk in the woods across the road from us. 2020: the year a nation discovered the simple joys of just going outside. It almost sounds a little whimsical now, doesn't it? The joy of simply being outside of your own house and discovering your local park. I had new eyes on the trees, the plants and the blue sky. It was springtime when I was in the trenches of sadness, and I will be forever thankful for the timing of it. Here's a tip: if you can, try to end your relationship in March. It really does give you a chance to have fantastic park time while you feel like a big steaming pile of dog turd.

So, for the five days a week when the kids were with me, we would walk around the woods in the sunshine. There were pathways I had never seen before and a tree swing that was in a magical clearing. All the park playgrounds had been closed, but this idyllic place was a special oasis. We found field mice, and a bird's nest, which we would visit each time and check for eggs as if we were in an Enid Blyton book . . . *The Terrific Three Get Divorced!*

One day, we walked around in the sunshine, doing the same walk as we always did. My son grabbed my hand and spontaneously said, 'Mummy, I am glad lockdown happened. These days have been the happiest of my life.' Oh, my darling boy. He was probably simply high on Haribo and thrilled I'd given up on homeschooling, but I squeezed his hand back, and the tears dropped out of my eyes. I felt the same. It was a strange mixed bag of emotions. I felt so far away from friends and family and from the life I once had, but I was so close to my children and was grateful we just did what we had to do. Even if it meant we had no teeth left and had to burn all our clothes by the end of it.

Like most people during lockdown, my 'messy months' wardrobe was basically leggings, tees and hoodies. I picked clothes that I knew I didn't have to change out of at night, or the next day, for that matter. The 48-hour collection. I replaced bras with crop tops or none at all, and I don't think I wore anything with a zip and a proper waist until I had an actual date in June. I also had a 'smoking jacket' by the front door, a cheap old puffer coat from Decathlon. If I needed to go outside at night for a sneaky fag, I put that on. It smelled like I had picked it out of the bin.

Getting dressed into normal clothes feels like a big transition when you're in the early stages. Samantha Baines, comedian and host of the *The Divorce Club* podcast, told me about her experience: 'I wrote a diary at the time, and I remember writing in it, "*put jeans on for the first time*" and that was a big marker of "*I'm going to be OK*" and then my sister made me leave the house. I was still in shock, but I started to do normal things, that made me think that life would carry on, but the shock was definitely there.'

I knew my health wasn't going to survive, but I wasn't prepared for the almighty crash I had in the first two months. Who knows if it was Covid or not, but for one week, I had to stay in bed with a horrific cough, and I was so weak I could barely move. The kids didn't want to leave me, so, as much as it killed me, I let my ex back into the house during the day, so he could look after them. IT WAS AWFUL. There were familiar sounds, and I heard him on work calls, like nothing had changed.

My cough and breathlessness stayed for another two months after that, and sometimes I would have moments where I couldn't get breath into my lungs. I would gasp for air and nearly pass out. And every time I had one of these coughing fits, I would wee everywhere – delightful! There were moments I thought I was going to die, which I know sounds incredibly dramatic, but on nights when I was in the house without the kids, I would sometimes wake up and be on my hands and knees trying to get air into my lungs. It was terrifying.

My interactions with my ex were so exhausting, too. One of the best decisions we made, though, was to have weekly therapy with the couples counsellor we had seen four years earlier. He at least knew the struggles we had been through, and I trusted him to support me – and I guess, us – through the separation process. These sessions weren't about getting us back together but rather helping us navigate the new life we were living apart. It also gave me one hour a week where I could communicate with my ex in a more sane and supported manner. In the beginning I was still texting him daily, mainly questions along the lines of

'What the fuck just happened?'

But I also sent long paragraphs telling him every feeling, thought and image that had crossed my mind. As the weeks went on, those texts became less and less, and we eventually ended the therapy after three months. Even though I just wanted to tell him to fuck off out of my life, I had to face the fact that, because of the children, I had to have a relationship with him, and I wanted to make sure I could eventually talk to him, albeit briefly, without wanting to either cry or punch him in the neck.

Family lawyer Laura Naser advises, 'You can't force someone to be nice to you and you can't force someone to be reasonable and rational, no matter how reasonable and rational you are and how much legal advice you have got. So if the communication between the two of you isn't working, then you have to look to third parties. Do you have a mutual friend or relation that you both respect and trust, and could they help? But that doesn't work for everyone, some people don't want to involve someone else, so then going to mediation can be really key. Sometimes it could just be going to a therapist, not to reconcile, but to have that space and other person to help you communicate'.

He knew our interactions were difficult for me. Pick-ups and drop-offs were incredibly triggering and hard. While I kept eye contact to a minimum and tried to make sure the kids were ready to go as soon as he arrived, it was still so painful to be near him. During the first six months, the kids went with him every weekend. He would collect them at 5pm on a Friday night and then come back Sunday night. So I had a whole weekend to rattle around in my house by myself.

And rattle I did. By the time I heard his car reverse out of the drive, I would have a bottle of wine in one hand and a lit cigarette in the other. And I didn't stop until I passed out, on both Friday and Saturday nights. Ellie and I were doing our Instagram comedy shows at 8.30pm on a Friday, so I had a few warm-up drinks and would then have a few more while we were performing. A local cocktails company would deliver us bottles of booze, and we gladly scoffed those. By the time the show had finished I was sozzled but also elated. I was doing the job I loved and cheering up people during a dark time with our daft jokes. Even though Ellie and I were in separate houses, I felt close to her too. I got the dopamine hits I craved and was buoyed by the admiration and my ability to make others happy. I could do this!

But then the crash would happen. The alcohol would help me sleep initially, but I would wake up at 3am needing to pee for England, thirsty and disorientated. The loneliness would set in. The bed felt big and the house empty and silent. As much as my children were full-on and exhausting at times, I missed them deeply when they were not with me. Learning to be by myself was going to take practice.

I also felt I had to manage the emotions of the loved ones who were trying to help me. The breakdown of our marriage hurt me and the kids, but its effects also spread to family and friends. One of the hardest things I had to do was tell my mum. Although I was in my forties, I of course still sought her love and approval. And as a mother myself, I knew that it was going to break her heart that she couldn't be with me. She would be beyond worried. I ended up waiting a whole week because I was more worried about her than I was about myself.

I finally summoned the strength and rang her on her mobile. The poor woman had enough on her plate – she was just about to go into the dentist. 'Hello, Helen!' she said excitedly. 'How are you and the children? All OK in London?'

'Mum, I'm so sorry, I have some sad news . . . My marriage is over, Mum. He's gone.'

'Oh, Helen. Oh, I am so sorry, oh you poor thing!' Her voice broke, and I heard her take a deep breath. And then I just broke down and sobbed and sobbed. I don't even know what I said after that. I was just so fucking sad. Not just for me, but for the hurt that was now rushing out to every corner of the world. I know I needed the support, but I hated the pain the news was causing others. Managing other people's expectations of you and their grief is overwhelming.

I spoke to Poorna Bell, the journalist and author of *Stronger: Changing Everything I Knew About Women's Strength*, who has written extensively about grief and surviving. When Poorna was in her deepest period of grief, she told me, 'I just thought there was no space for anything that wasn't useful, or going to give me comfort, or help me to heal. This was about knowing who I needed and wanted to be around, and the type of interactions that I would have with people, and really ring-fencing and safeguarding myself, in a way that I had never ever done before.

'So a classic example were people's weddings – previously I would have thought it was unthinkable to say to someone, "I'm not going to your wedding," but I didn't go to anyone's wedding for about two and a half years. And the first wedding that I went to I was really ready for that and I didn't have to explain . . . This was the other thing as well: depending on the scenario, you do owe someone an explanation, but there was a lot of stuff where I just thought, "I don't need to explain my thoughts and feelings around this," and that then taps into things like being aware of how much mental and emotional energy you actually give, unthinkingly, to people.

'If I have to sit down and then explain the complicated thought processes around all of that, to someone – and I don't know how emotionally intelligent that person is; I don't know how they're going to react to it – so not only do I have to talk about something difficult, I then have to manage their reaction around it. I'm like, "I'm not doing that."

'And, actually, if I don't manage my own boundaries, if I don't figure out what I want to say no to, if I constantly say yes, because I want to be liked, or I'm worried that other people are going to be disappointed, there's no end point to that. You can't behave in a certain way because you're constantly pre-empting people's disappointment – they're not going to appreciate I sacrificed my mental well-being to come to something I didn't want to, because they have got their own boundaries that they say no around.'

Knowing my own boundaries and getting deep into the sadness of it all was hard to avoid. Everything was a trigger in those early days. It could be anything from hearing love songs on the radio or glancing at my wedding ring to seeing loved-up couples in the park, or just those bloody Timehop things on social media – no, I don't want to be reminded that I was on holiday in Italy with him in 2018. Fuck off, Facebook. And some mornings I would wake up crying. The tears just wouldn't stop. I couldn't just happy myself out of this, and I was struggling.

One of my biggest breakdowns came about a month in. It was his birthday, and the kids wanted to make him a cake and have him come to the house. I have no idea why I agreed to this, but I think I was on autopilot and just went with it. Of course I would do anything to make the children happy. I even gave him a present. I went through our box of photos and took out all the pictures of him and his family and collected them in a folder and then put two photos of the kids in frames and wrapped them up nicely. Perhaps I wanted him to see what he had destroyed; perhaps I needed to let go. Each photo brought me pain. I kept asking myself how I had spent over twenty years with this man. I looked at his face in the pictures, trying to see the man I used to love, but he looked different, as if he had morphed into someone else.

We set the table with cake and candles, and then he came into the house and I felt like I was going to throw up. I went for a walk down to the park and left them all together having a jolly time. The kids looked so happy. I knew I had done the right thing, but that didn't mean it was easy. As soon as I stepped out of the front door I was already feeling short of breath, and my eyes were foggy. I took some gins in a tin and a packet of fags, and then I sat on a park bench and drank, smoked and rubbed my face until it stung.

Getting comfortable with crying, and especially just spontaneously in public, was something I had to work hard at. I asked Anna Mathur why tears are so important: 'Every tear changes the body biologically and chemically, and crying is good; it's healing and beneficial and it changes things. You'll never have that tear again, because every tear, in the little tear lake, is gone now.'

In both Australian and British cultures, we are actively encouraged not to be sad. When we are, the majority of us don't know how to deal with it. Aussie culture is heavily macho, and emotions are generally suppressed under our 'No worries, mate' attitude, while the stiff-upper-lip approach still reigns in Old Blighty. Growing up, I distinctly remember boys especially being told not to cry. If anyone was seen crying at school, they would be teased for being a 'baby'. When I was a teenager, I went through a terrible time being bullied at school. I was incredibly depressed and moped around the house under a cloud of misery. One night I was having another rant at my mum about how much I hated school, and she just snapped, grabbed me by the shoulders and shouted, 'Why can't you just be happy?' I was shocked. She had never done anything like that before, and hasn't since.

I immediately yelled back at her, 'Because I'm so sad, Mum!' It felt like my sadness was wrong, and an inconvenience. Back then I was processing rejection and being unloved by my friends at school, and this is the sadness I was experiencing again as an adult.

While being sad has had a bad reputation, our attitudes about it are changing. Author Helen Russell, after spending eight years researching happiness, decided to delve into the opposite emotion and recently released the book *How to be Sad*. I asked her what she had discovered researching sadness globally. 'One of the things that struck me time and time again,' she said, 'was how phobic people were of being sad. They were so desperate to be happy. But you're never going to be truly happy if you're afraid of being sad.'

She thought for a minute and continued: 'I think often we don't do hard things because we are scared of feeling sad, but sadness is normal. It's a message; it's trying to tell us something. If we stay busy all the time, trying to distract ourselves so we don't have to think about things so much, then that's not really living. And we have to sit with the sadness, even though it's hard. It's worth it.'

'So how do you be sad?' I asked.

'I think first of all it's not fighting it and then it's allowing time, because it does take longer than anyone hopes or expects. And it's not apologising for it, and I think that's a really big one. I think as a people-pleasing Brit, someone who's been brought up to be a good girl, there's this sense that we have to apologise for our feelings. That has to stop. And then it's sitting with it and talking about it. For years it was thought that a sign of strength was not talking about things, and that what you don't talk about can't hurt you, and we know now that the opposite is true. We have to talk about these things, not necessarily in a cryptic Facebook post, but you know, to people in real life, and to a therapist if you feel that that's necessary. Obviously if normal sadness tips over into something more serious then of course you go and see your doctor.

'But there's evidence to suggest that there is a tendency to pathologise a lot of normal sadness because we are so unused to experiencing it. We're even teaching kids that normal sadness is not OK, saying, "I just want you to be happy," and that puts a lot of pressure on them. So I think it's key to normalise sadness from a really young age and talk to kids about it and allow ourselves to experience it, to be kinder to ourselves when we're feeling like that.'

I realised that I had done exactly that with my own children, in the early days after the separation. I kept saying things like, 'Mummy will always make you happy!' or 'I want this to be a happy house of three!' or the big lie, 'Don't worry, kids, Mummy is happy, everything is OK.' Of course I said those things because I just *wanted* them to be true. I thought that, by protecting the kids from hurt, I was doing something heroic and good. But now I know we all just have to let it out.

Unlike when I was a young mother, now that I was in my forties and less of an uptight know-it-all, I gladly took advice from anyone and everyone. I wasn't just going to trust my instincts on this or feel my way through it. This bit was dirty, and painful. I had no idea what I was doing and needed guidance.

I was lucky that I have two good friends who are amazing psychologists, and they both gave me two pieces of advice in that first month of madness that have stuck with me and were like mantras in the early days. I would say the same to anyone in the same boat as me.

Baz told me, 'To get outta hell, you've just gotta get through the shit.' Meaning sit with your feelings, face them, ugly cry in the bath and get all those thoughts out.

And Colette said, 'You're allowed to be angry. Scream, yell, go out into a field and smash things if you want. You have to allow yourself to feel this anger.' Anger? I didn't want to be angry. I didn't do angry. I was far more Kate Middleton than Courtney Love. Anger felt like a weakness, and not a way to release pain.

But in fact there was a lot to be angry about. I was angry that he had let me live a lie for so long, that he thought it was fine for him to treat me that way, that I had been robbed of happiness, and that I was always so flipping faithful to him. I kept thinking back to the year before when I had a month at the Edinburgh Fringe festival. I could have fucked a different person every night, but I was such a goodie two-shoes! Damn it!

While I confronted the anger I had felt, there was this other big bag of crap that came up while going through this period – all the negative things that I had just accepted in my relationship before the separation. The little comments, huffs or sighs of disappointment or annoyance, or just those feelings of not being good enough, were toxic and bitter. The conversations that would start with things like, *How many times have I told you not to do that?* or *I know you're not going to understand this, but* . . . and *Why is it so hard for you to do this?* And I am sure I did my equal share in return – I was far from perfect and probably really irritating. But it is remarkable when you get out of a relationship that has spectacularly soured, and you look back on it with fresh eyes, and see all the bad behaviours you accepted or contributed. And hopefully won't ever accept, or repeat, again.

Getting into a rut of just putting up with shitty behaviours and habits is something I was guilty of, and when I was married I couldn't see a way out of it. Anyway, how do you know what is just a niggle rather than something that needs to be addressed?

Arabella Weir told me, 'Never accept behaviour from a partner that you wouldn't accept from your best friend. That is, would you let your best mate sit at the dinner table and say, "Oh, God, why did you cook the broccoli like this?" or "Why did you buy Chardonnay? You know I hate Chardonnay."?'

Ouch! When she said these words, I felt exposed. I had just accepted the everyday papercuts, and while each of them seemed insignificant, added up together, they made for a gaping wound.

My anger needed to come out. I got in touch with Anna Mathur. I wanted some calming words and her perspective on rage and anger. I asked her how to deal with anger at such a raw time. And why do women fear anger so much?

Anna replied, 'I think there's always fear in anger, so when you are angry, it's good to ask yourself what you are actually fearful of? There's probably something in you that feels threatened, and I think it can be helpful just to identify it. For some people, rage is a very physical, *live* feeling, and to have to hold it in for long is challenging – it ends up coming out sideways, like steam from a pressure cooker, with the kids, or with a friend, or with a family member who says something well-meaning but slightly irritating. Acknowledging that anger is important. Sometimes we do have to hold rage in, for instance in front of the kids, but there is a time to let it go, to allow yourself to just feel it. And, if the rage is a physical thing, ask yourself, what do I want to do with my body? What do I want to do with my hands? Do I want to punch something or somebody? What if you got a picture of your ex on a pillow and punched that? What about writing it down, boxing, running, racing through the woods, just going out and screaming. Ask yourself how you can respect the sensation and find a constructive or non-harmful way to actually let it be what it is. You have to find opportunities to release it.

'We're so hard-wired, culturally, to be nice, to be good, to push rage down, but sometimes to respect yourself is to notice the injustice of it all. We want to avoid those feelings, but sometimes it's about encouraging them because beyond those feelings is where the good stuff is.

'I think there's real fear that if we feel rage, we'll never stop. But it's a feeling, and, like everything, it passes, and the only way we can build trust in an emotion is by letting it be, by growing in confidence that it does pass and that there are better things at the end of it. The only way through is through. It's like grief. No, it is grief: you ask yourself, *Why me, why them, why did they leave me? This isn't fair and I hate it* – and that's a really healthy yet uncomfortable feeling. Because there isn't always an answer to these kinds of questions. We try desperately to find reasons, and sometimes the rage comes with the recognition that it was just point-blank unfair and shit and undeserved and that it wasn't about you.'

Anna had encapsulated everything I felt and feared in a 20-minute conversation. I had feared the anger, and I had feared what I would be like if I did actually let it all out. There was so much rage inside of me, which I felt could only be resolved by answers from him. But it was all down to me. He had done his part, and now it was time for me to act.

So I decided to give anger a go. And, if you're new to anger like I was, it does seem like a big step. How do you process a toxic relationship or years of hurt and betrayal? Well, turns out there are lots of satisfying and healthy ways to do it. I found playing really angry break-up music and yelling out the lyrics incredibly fun and cathartic. There is a song by Ben Folds Five called 'Song for the Dumped', which I think I listened to at least 6,000 times, along with Tina Arena's 'Chains' and Martha Wainwright's 'Bloody Mother Fucking Asshole'. All excellent for rage release.

Getting outside and going for a stomp in the woods, or just around the block thinking about how much I hated my ex and what a bastard he had been, was also excellent. There were a few eureka moments. Once, after sending numerous ALL CAPS texts to him, I put down my phone, and, for the first time ever, yelled, 'I really fucking hate you!' It was an extraordinary release. On another particularly bad day, I went to the park across the road and yelled out 'CUUUUUUUUUUUUUUUNNNNT' a couple of times, and it made me feel remarkably better.

One of the glorious things about my double act with Ellie, as opposed to a marriage, is that we naturally divide tasks and are an excellent match for each other, with different strengths and weaknesses. So when I was in the pits of sadness and could only feel hurt and rejection, I outsourced my anger to Ellie. She could see how broken I was, and she was FURIOUS. She had brilliant, unbridled, female rage. I would ring her and tell her all my feelings, and she would release the most glorious swears: 'That's fucking outrageous!'; 'You don't deserve this bullshit'; 'This is bloody disgraceful.' Every divorcee needs a random insult generator in their life. Ellie was mine.

While I had tried to keep things at least civil between my ex and me in person, there was one almighty phone call when I released all the rage that had been building. We had been discussing when we should start to proceed with the official divorce. I just snapped. 'I DO NOT WANT YOU TO BE MY HUSBAND ANY MORE. I WANT THIS MARRIAGE OVER WITH. AND I WANT IT DONE.' Roooooaaaaarrrrrrrrrr. I was electrified. I was powerful. I have never felt so alive.

I was fucking furious. HELLO, ANGER, THERE YOU ARE. COME ON IN.

So I let the tears flow, I screamed in the park, and I gradually found peace in being broken and bra-less. This time of crying and rage was part of becoming stronger. With each deep breath, I got closer and closer to moving on. While I hadn't chosen to separate, I was bloody determined the new life foisted on me was going to be BETTER; That is was going to be fantastic.

I was going to get happier and rebuild myself.

Watch out, world, I was coming back.

Things I have learnt going through shock, grief, sadness and anger

- Don't fight the sadness. Allow yourself to get right into it. Have days listening to sad songs if you need, and, if you can, either get friends to bring you food or live off takeaways.

- Don't put any expectations or deadlines on your grief. And, for God's sake, don't compare yourself to others going through separation; your journey to recovery will not be the same.

- Your anger won't last forever, and neither will the tears, so accept them when they arrive. Find the best ways you can process these feelings, whether it is exercise, shouting in the park, writing shit down or singing and dancing to angry songs. Enjoy the power and energy of it too.

- If you can afford it, find a good therapist that you are happy with, at least for the early stages of separation, just so you have that support available to you once a week. Or, find a couple of close friends you can really be yourself with.

- Your sadness doesn't and won't define you. You are not a sad person; you are just going through a fucking sad time.

- Also, eat lasagne. Lots of lasagne.

4

Moving Forward and Getting Happy

One morning, three months after we had separated, something happened, which I'd thought was impossible. I woke up and didn't feel sad. In fact, I felt a *little* bit better. It was completely out of the blue. I hadn't done anything different the night before; there had been no realignment of my chakras nor some spectacular existential epiphany. I'd just opened my eyes and was OK. The sun was shining through my curtains.

I went downstairs and made myself a coffee, then just stood there in my kitchen staring at the messy table and all the washing on the drying rack, feeling like me again. I had an odd sense of peace. My life was going to be all right.

After those messy months, day by day, I slowly began to enjoy having the house to the three of us. Instead of the jolts of pain and sorrow, I was starting to get little buzzes of happiness. It was as if my life had always been a wonderful garden, but my ex had been a big old tree overshadowing it. When he left, the sunshine was able to come in, and bit by bit the flowers began to bloom.

Really random awakenings and realisations would hit me. It was during dinner one night when it suddenly occurred to me that no one was going to make a negative comment about how I cooked my pasta (yes, I like it soft, OK?) or tell me off for having the heating up too high or sigh if I farted and found it funny (farting *is* hilarious). I found immense pleasure in making lists of things that fucked me off about him; it was petty and puerile and I highly recommend it. 'I won't ever have to see his nail clippings again!' I thought one morning. 'I don't have to listen to the noises he makes as he eats an apple.' I WAS FREEEEEEEEEE!

In this new phase, I discovered that even the most mundane tasks felt like treats. A trip to the supermarket was like going to fucking Disneyland. The kids and I would skip along, buying Custard Creams, Crunchy Nut Cornflakes and Ben and Jerry's ice cream like we were in our first week of university and had just got our student loans. And, as we were in lockdown and there weren't many other places to go, our trips to get snacks became our days out.

One sunny day, when my son and I were out walking along our local high street, he wistfully said, 'We have so many lovely memories in that Sainsbury's. It's our happy place, Mummy!', which made my heart sing, and we had a little hug. How delicious that we had made doing everyday tasks together into something to be cherished. See what buying shitloads of Chocolate Bourbons can do?

Other simple pleasures were having kitchen discos, watching endless episodes of *RuPaul's Drag Race* and performing our own 'lockdown realness' catwalks. Music and dancing became integral to all of us healing. We sang the *Frozen 2* soundtrack on repeat. The kids were both learning an instrument, my son the cornet and my daughter the flute, and I started to play the piano again too. I had learnt for ten years as a child and teen, and could sight-read fairly well. One day I just sat down and banged out some tunes and felt alive. I learnt some cheesy musical classics that we could sing along to and downloaded pop songs that I could belt out when the kids weren't around. I was reconnecting with a part of me that had been buried for over two decades, and, by unearthing it, I felt like a teenager again.

Just small moments of happiness can hit you when you least expect it. For Helen Serafinowicz, comedy writer and producer of the TV series *Motherland,* she told me that, 'shortly after he left, the dog did that bum wipe thing on the kitchen floor, leaving an "S" shape. Me and the kids laughed so much I thought I was going to collapse. I remembered how we hadn't laughed like that for so fucking long. All the worry and anxiety lifted. I felt like Rocky running up those steps.'

And for TV presenter and NHS doctor, Dr Ranj Singh, his moment of joy after becoming single was, 'being able to go for a poo completely naked, with the bathroom door wide open, the music blaring, and a glass of champers in my hand. That has made me realise that no man's gonna come between me and my happy dumps!'

And it wasn't just how I felt that started to change; I began to look different, too. My eyes were more sparkly, and my skin began to shine. Friends kept saying, 'Helen, divorce has made you look younger!' It's not that I had changed my favourite Aldi face cream; my happiness was making me glow. I remember one day I was in the supermarket and a woman I know yelled across the aisle at me, 'Hey Helen, you look great. Have you lost weight?'

'No,' I answered, 'but I did shed a husband. That was quite a bit of weight to lose.' Twelve stone, to be precise. I felt so much lighter not carrying him or his expectations around with me any more. And I had gone from desperately holding on to a life partner, to feeling elated being by myself and not even remotely interested in finding someone new.

Not wanting to get straight into another relationship is very common for older women who have been in a long-term relationship. I spoke to the journalist and author Francesca Specter, who has written extensively about the joys of being alone in her book, *Alonement: How To Be Alone & Absolutely Own It*. Francesca said, 'It's interesting because women are typically so much better at being happily single, and men are much more likely to remarry within the five years after their first marriage, whereas women aren't and that's through choice. There was a survey conducted by *The Sunday Times*[2] which found women on average don't feel the same urgency to remarry; and I think this is because – after having devoted those years of your life, as a partner, as a parent, to other people's needs – you don't feel the need to then effectively become a caregiver for yet another person. Men get very used to having someone there. While there are still obstacles for women to overcome around being happily single – for instance, there's a shortage of role models out there and we're still trying to throw off the sexist Bridget Jones/spinster connotations of yesteryear – men often struggle more because they don't have the social networks that women have, and it's harder for them to find emotional support that a partner

2 Fleur Britten, 'Meet the new breed of happy divorcee: women who are empowered, positive and thrilled to be single', *Style* Magazine, *The Sunday Times,* Sunday September 23 2018. https://www.thetimes.co.uk/article/meet-the-new-breed-of-happy-divorcee-women-who-are-empowered-positive-and-thrilled-to-be-single-7skzg3k8s

would give them. So, even while it's not necessarily portrayed in the media, I think women are a lot more capable of being single and thriving, bolstered by these wide social support systems. Especially in later life.'

The divine happiness I feel these days as a single woman is what I expected to receive from being married. It has been such a joy to discover that I can feel jolly and fulfilled all alone. I'm floating around in an infatuated state with myself and this new life, and I now skip through my day instead of dragging my heels. I dance like no one's watching, sing eighties power ballads like no one's listening, cook like no one's complaining and stack my dishwasher like no one's criticising. But crucially, I no longer spend my time waiting for 'better times' or 'easier moments' or to feel more love, or more of anything, really, because it is all just here. My body now bubbles with possibility, and I feel giddy about all the things that lie ahead of me rather than mourning what I left behind. Some days, I just want to run down the street shouting, 'I FUCKING LOVE BEING SINGLE!'

Getting my happy back over this year has taken time and a lot of therapy and crying. Going through a trauma isn't just about facing the pain of that experience. Oh no, it brings up all the crap that you have EVER experienced and lays it all out on display, like at a car-boot sale of misery. Once I started talking to my therapist, Gill, it was all there for us both to look at and work through: 'Oh, hey there, school bullying; nice to see you again body hang-ups; father issues . . . great to have you back!' Week by week in therapy, I opened up old wounds and faced hard truths about my past.

Going back through painful times was exhausting, but it also gave me the chance to find moments of strength that I had hidden. As I mentioned, I'd been badly bullied as a teenager. I grew up in a small country town in Australia, where frankly I didn't fit in or belong. I was a classic dork: I loved musicals; surrealist art; wearing charity-shop clothes; and debating. Surely I was just asking for it with those life choices? My dad, who had previously been a vicar, had now changed professions, and was a teacher at my high school, and I am sure it was difficult for him to make a fuss about what was happening to me.

After spending over a year feeling miserable, I decided that one day I couldn't stand being sad any more. I had taken up an evening art class (yes, I was *that* kind of fourteen-year-old) where I had met a girl my age called Loretta. She was sparkly and fun and went to a school I hadn't heard of before. She told me how happy she was there and that, even though it took an hour to get there on an early-morning bus, it was totally worth it. Was this school and this new friend a chance for me to escape?

Without telling my parents, I secretly rang the school and arranged to meet the principal to talk about transferring in the new year. Like the nerd I was, I pulled together all the information about uniforms, buses and timetables and pitched it to Mum and Dad. They thankfully agreed – they were probably just as exhausted by my misery as I was – and we all went along for that first meeting, where I burst into tears and told the kind principal how sad and bullied I was. He was thoughtful and listened, and said I would be very welcome at the school and could start in the new year. I spent the next three years at that school flourishing and being insanely happy. I adored my new friends, I excelled in my school work, and I felt loved and accepted. But none of this would have happened if I hadn't made that change myself, if I hadn't decided I deserved to be happy or if I had just expected others to make me better. I could have sat around all day and blamed everyone else or been bitter about what life had given me, but I didn't. My fourteen-year-old self rocked; she was strong, and she had the courage to turn her life around. And I had found her again.

During therapy, it became apparent that transforming my life wasn't just about saying yes to new things but also becoming better at saying no to stuff. At one stage my therapist told me to practise getting better at saying no by looking in the mirror every day and saying it twenty times. I am a total pro at this now.

Even just saying what I really wanted had become hard for me. When I was with Ellie, she'd sometimes ask what I wanted for lunch, and I'd say, 'I don't mind, whatever you like.'

'You're allowed to choose, Helen!' She understood that I was afraid to say what I wanted. I now realised I *was* frightened; my relationship with her was so precious that it felt like it was an exquisite gift, and I just wanted her to always be happy, and be happy with me. This, of course, was a product of my low self-esteem coupled with years of being worn down by my ex's criticisms. Sure, this is not uncommon in relationships; you get to a point where everything about the other person annoys you. And admittedly I was guilty of it, too. But it was things like, the hotel I'd picked for our holiday wasn't quite right, or the towels I'd bought for the bathroom weren't good enough – that kind of thing. It was surprising how he could twist things to be my fault – once he blamed me for making him burp, because I had apparently put the wrong ingredients in his dinner. Obviously I had made him Yotam Ottolenghi's Mediterranean Belch Tagine. After years of this, I felt that if things fucked up, I was to blame. I am sure that, because things had gotten so bad between us, he probably felt the same.

While being a people-pleaser is very much part of who I am, I have now discovered that always trying to make others happy isn't good for me, or them either. I spoke with the writer Rebecca Cox, who runs the social media account @singlemotheredit, about what this actually means. We both agreed we were guilty of it, but Rebecca said that she had heard something that made her change her mind about her behaviours.

'I listened to a podcast recently,' she told me, 'and something resonated with me so much that I wrote it down: "People-pleasing is dishonesty". People-pleasers think they're being a good person 'cos they're trying to make other people happy all the time: "Oh, you know I just wanted to make you happy . . ." No, actually . . . you're lying to yourself, you're being dishonest and I was like, "that hurts, but it's true" . . . 'cos I do it on dates, and I'm literally, "how can I make myself attractive to this guy?" . . . You have to be yourself; otherwise you're just gonna be in this position again. If you just mould yourself into what others want from you all the time, which is what is expected of women, you will never then have something that is worth leaving this amazing situation of being a single mum for. I will not be giving up being a single mum for anything less than pretty much exceptional.'

Those words strongly resonated with me. If I am honest, I had been dishonest with both my ex and myself about how happy I was. And I had spent a lifetime being a people-pleaser and trying to find my own happiness through others. The separation had given me this chance to really address not only my strengths but my faults, too.

Going through a break-up feels like it should weaken or diminish you, but, for many of us, it does the opposite. Rosie Wilby, author of *The Breakup Monologues,* told me, 'The good bits of each break-up are that it makes you stronger and makes you better equipped for life in general. There have been surveys where people who have gone through a break-up report many positives, including their ability to make better choices going forward.' She added, 'Through break-up I have gained an insight into myself and an ability to negotiate to argue better, in a peaceful and calm manner. You learn communication and listening skills.'

Personal gains like these started to contribute to my happiness. I began to feel a greater strength in my choices, and better at asking for what I want. So getting happy wasn't about simply going back to the 'old Helen' nor inventing a brand-new one. I had to slowly retrieve and stitch back together the fragments of myself that lay in a mess on the floor. A sort of Frankenstein's monster, but one with great tits, an Aussie accent and fabulous earrings.

As I gained confidence, I felt ownership over my new life and home. To mark the beginning of our new family of three, I organised for a local photographer to take some portraits of us outside the house. I had removed pictures of my ex, so I wanted to fill the walls with new memories. And bit by bit, I began to make the house feel totally ours, too. I didn't have much money, but I bought cheery cushion covers and a cheap rug for the lounge, and I started to throw out crap I didn't need in the house. I felt LIBERATED. I daydreamed about what it might look like in the future. I could paint the kitchen pink if I wanted to, buy a fuck-off huge bath and put up a poster of a shirtless Idris Elba in the loo ... anything I

GET DIVORCED, BE HAPPY

goddamn wanted to. And what was even better than doing things he would have hated, or disapproved of, was not thinking about him AT ALL.

Once I had made the switch from focusing on what I was missing out on to what I was gaining from being divorced, then these gleeful moments just kept flooding in. Even when there were times of sadness, or when I felt overwhelmed by being a single parent, they quickly became points of pride and resilience.

For Natalie Lee, who runs the Instagram account @stylemesunday, it was the sense of freedom that gave her most joy after her separation. 'One of the weird things about being single,' she said, 'is that I don't have to ask anyone for anything. I don't have to have somebody put me off anything. I can just do it. That has been revolutionary just to have that autonomy. That's been lovely, making my home really cosy, and a lovely place to be, and exactly how I want it. I was really adamant about carving out that time for me to be heard, basically. I think that one of my major issues with my relationship is that I didn't feel heard. I didn't feel like my needs were being met, so therapy was good; it was time to focus on me and have somebody listen to me and talk through things. And just making those sort of choices, for you and you alone. Journaling has been good. Exercise, dancing, and I also love running; I've now got a running machine in my kitchen . . . just those little kind of things; choosing yourself, really.'

Knowing what makes you happy and having the opportunity to fill your life with everything that you love without compromise is just the biggest gift separation can give you. And also, having a good laugh about all the shit bits is incredibly important.

Having a good sense of humour, and just naturally wanting to see the funny side of life, helped me greatly in recovering from my trauma and heartbreak. I spoke with Kathy Lette, the Australian author and legend, who has for decades entertained audiences and readers with her sharp wit, asking her, 'Why is humour so helpful during our dark times?'

Kathy said, 'Humour allows you to strap a giant shock absorber to your brain. If you can laugh at something, it takes the sting out of it. I think there is a big difference between male and female humour. My male friends tend to tell set jokes: "An Aussie bloke, an Irishman and a Jewish fella walk into a bar. 'What is this?' asks the bartender, 'Some kind of joke?'"

'But women's humour is much more cathartic, candid, confessional and self-deprecating. And it's also incredibly funny. That's because women have what I call a "Black Belt in Tongue-fu". Linguists tell us that women use, on average, about five hundred extra words in our daily vocabulary. Men may be physically stronger, but women can disarm a bully with a quick bit of quip lash. It's also interesting to note that anthropologists maintain that women, in all cultures on the planet, laugh more often than men; especially in all-female groups. Why is that? Well, laughing at life's adversities is just the way women cope. We'd never get through our darker days without a good laugh with our human wonder bras. And women do have a lot of darker days because, generally speaking, we are the carers. We care for aged relatives, ill siblings, fragile friends and our children – no matter what their needs – some of which are special. Which is definitely true in my case. My son is autistic, which can be incredibly stressful, demoralising and demanding, but being able to laugh, sometimes through tears, with my sisters and my

girlfriends is what keeps me resilient and sane. OK . . .
relatively sane!"

Having a sense of humour definitely kept me sane, and
having the chance to share that on social media played a big
part in my recovery and happiness. Through telling my stories
of my newly single life, I started to feel a sense of real purpose
and a responsibility to honestly reflect my experience publicly.
I loved that I could quickly connect with other women going
through similar milestones, but also just show everyone,
single or not, how happy life can be on your own.

Whether it was sharing how I ended up washing the same
load of smelly clothes three times because I didn't get round
to hanging them out, or that I had to take both my kids with
me to the shop to get milk at 8pm because I was alone, I
wanted to document the day-to-day realities of singledom.
This wasn't a 'Why me?' thing; it was 'Look what I can do'.
And I loved that people in the same boat shared their thoughts,
providing advice and encouragement to me and others.
Feeling that connection, especially when we weren't allowed
to hug or see each other, felt nourishing, and it motivated me
to want to be a champion of single mothers everywhere.

The joy I got from giving to others through my work was
helping me become happier. As Helen Russell told me, 'There
is so much evidence around now saying that doing something
for someone else is a really good thing to do when you're
feeling sad. There's a lot of studies now and years of research
into "warm glow giving"; so either donating to charity, or
volunteering, or helping someone else in some way. It's almost
like, if you just do you when you're sad, you're not going
to feel much better, but if you help someone else, that can
really help.'

There were lots of moments that felt like steps forward, moving on from being a married woman to being a very happily single one. The most significant event, however, was on a warm mini-break weekend in July.

After spending months inside the same house, staring at the same TV and living in the same PJs, I was given the chance to escape by my kind friends Huey and Joseph. They offered Ellie and me a few nights away at their gorgeous cottage in Kent. We invited Ellie's best mate Jessie to come along too.

On the first night, after many wines, we decided that as a symbolic gesture I should finally remove my wedding ring and be free of my marriage. As I was at least three stone heavier than on my wedding day, my fingers had expanded somewhat since, and it was going to take a lot of assistance. We used a bottle of olive oil, butter, soap and even some toothpaste at one point. We filmed all our various failed attempts and shared them on social media. Our feed exploded with women suggesting a multitude of solutions, but the one that stood out was that I should take myself off to the nearest fire station.

So the next day, we three women embarked on an adventure to the Kent Fire Station. It was going to take us an hour to walk there, but we were charged with determination and excitement. We arrived and knocked on the door, but there was no answer. Then we went round the back and knocked some more. Our hearts began to sink a little. Was this epic journey all for nought? Then suddenly the front door creaked open and a strapping fireman answered it. Ellie fronted up to him and said, 'My friend can't get her wedding ring off. Can you cut it off?'

He nodded politely and said, 'Of course we can, come in.' We all went giddy and giggled like teenagers.

Sadly, we were told we couldn't film the event, so you'll just have to believe what happened next. He sat me down, and then, one by one, three more hunky firemen appeared to help me with this ceremonial event. One held a power saw, one held a bag of ice to try to reduce the swelling, and another had a bottle of Fairy Liquid to lubricate my finger. I'm not sure what the other did, but he was cute, and that definitely helped matters.

They slid a small metal plate between my finger and the ring and began to saw through the band. It was a slow process, because the platinum was so hard, and the diamond cutter would heat up the metal and start to feel like it was burning me. So we fell into a rhythm of hot power saw followed by daubing with ice. Honestly it was one of the most erotic things that has ever happened to me, and if this book ever gets made into a film, I want to cast the four men as themselves.

Eventually the saw cut through the band. Two firemen encircled me (social-distancing was long out the window by this point, but of course there were still masks); and, with a set of pliers each, they tried to gently pull my ring open. They iced my finger again, dripped the soapy lubey liquid on my finger, held my hand above my heart to reduce the swelling, and then, finally, my wedding ring slid off my finger for the first time in ten years. That's right: it took one man to put it on and four to remove it. Phwoar . . .

Sorry, I just need a moment, readers.

Ah, now then. Where was I? Oh yes. We took a magnificent photo of the three of us outside the fire station and shared our beaming faces on Instagram. Comments came flying at us from everywhere, cheering us on. I felt the warm embrace of thousands of women, all of whom knew how significant this moment was. I was buoyed by their love and support and knew this wasn't just for me, but for so many women who had walked this path. Obviously, without the firemen, mind you.

Having my wedding ring removed was not only symbolic; it was energising. I kept looking at the red mark left by it and felt renewed. It was important in breaking free of my identity as mother/wife and becoming a single mother, and a single woman. Having these two new identities connected me to new groups of women and gave me the opportunity to create new stories. While I had always worked hard in my career during my relationship, I now felt even more free to pursue creative sides of me and get my mojo back.

Rosie Wilby told me what I was experiencing was 'break-up energy', which, she said, is 'something like an energising force we feel after the chaos, and the heartbreak has dissipated a little bit, and we suddenly feel more present in the world. We feel more alive and more connected.' She told me that it was definitely the time when she had done her best creative work, writing books or shows and starting up new projects. 'And I do feel I am smiling at people and going out with friends and connecting with people more. I really love break-up me!' she said. I too felt that 'break-up me' was starting to shine brightly.

Becoming more sexual was also part of this transformation, as I will discuss in far more detail than you might care for a little later in the book. Regaining a sense of my sexuality was encouraged by my new love of lingerie. Lots and lots of lingerie. You know, the stuff with lace, stringy bits and pants that give you thrush if you wear them for more than 27 minutes. One of the first bits of advice I got from a friend about restoring my self-confidence was to take photos of myself in nice bras and pants. This was a new experience for me. I had worn the same type of big over-the-tummy wonderful cotton M&S pants and greying bras for the past decade. I did once buy some G-strings in my twenties, but I prefer pants that feel like they are hugging rather than fingering me. To be honest, the big M&S stuff is still what I wear most days, but I now also have a drawer full of sexy things that I can put on if I want to give myself a boost, for a date, say, or if I simply feel like looking a bit like a Christmas gammon covered in tinsel.

So, on the weekends when I was alone, I would pop on some polyester sex strings, whack on some lipstick and badly applied blusher and get out the iPhone. For every 150 pictures I took, there were about three that I'd be happy to post. I learnt that angles are a very important thing when trying to get that 'sexy shot', and taking a photo from above does wonders for making a double chin magically disappear, but it isn't about that at all. Seeing yourself as desirable is the real value.

I hadn't been single for nearly twenty-two years, and it had been almost that long since I'd felt desired sexually. To feel that tingle of self-love and self-worth that had been missing for so long was electrifying.

As the first official part of divorce was approaching, I decided to mark the occasion of my decree nisi by buying a new dress. Of course it was going to be a Westwood. That size 12 wedding dress had a corset, hooks and zips and literally shaped me, hoisting up my tits and squeezing in my waist so I couldn't eat. As my friend Taryn had said at the time, 'You don't wear that dress, it wears you.' But for my divorce, I bought a size 18 dress. It was long and stretchy, draped around my curves and didn't change my shape; it just showed it off. Yes, I was imperfect, and, yes, I was older and definitely wider, but I was free to be my glorious self.

Things that helped me get happy after separation

- Making a list of all the things you are free to do now without compromise or judgement. Anything from eating pasta in the bath, to painting your front door bright yellow. Do things that you did before you were in a couple, and/or start something new. Enjoy this new life ahead of you.

- It sounds silly, but make sure you leave the house every day and go for a walk, even if it is just to buy more wine and biscuits. Just getting some fresh air and exercise does wonders for your mood.

- Treat yourself to a new set of underwear and PJs. It is amazing how just a few new little things can cheer you up.

- Have a disco for one and make a set list of your favourite tracks and dance to your heart's content.

- Buy new things for your home, even if it just a new cushion cover, or a framed photo of Chris Hemsworth; you know, stuff that makes you smile.

- Organise a dinner party with all your closest friends and get everyone to bring some food, like a grown-up picnic, but indoors, and with wine!

5

When Four Become Three: Becoming a Single Parent and Telling the Kids

When I said I never wanted to get divorced, I think a large part of this was that I never wanted to be a single parent. The portrait of 'single mother' is one that has been poisoned with negative imagery and language for what seems like an eternity. Similar to mothers in general, the notion that we are all sad, dishevelled, not coping, chaotic and, at worst, husband-stealing banshees, is outdated and only feeds into the narrative that we are unable to survive without a man, or in fact alone. And this is bullshit.

However, I have to be honest: there was a part of me that believed the lies, and in the beginning, I was scared of what lay ahead of me. I wrongly assumed that single parenting would involve too much of a compromise of the life that I lived and loved. I worried about things like, how would I afford it, or basic things like, how would I go to the supermarket? How do you manage two children's school schedules? What if the kids were sick? What if I needed to work and couldn't get childcare? How do I change the lightbulbs in the bathroom? How would I just financially survive? Would the kids be OK? Would I be lonely with just me and them? But as I discovered over the course of this year, I had little to worry about, and a whole lot to cherish and shout loudly and proudly about.

I use the term single parent for myself, as I was told by the single-parent charity, Gingerbread, that if you have your children more than half the time, then you're a 'single parent', but I know these terms mean different things for different people, so, for the purposes of this chapter and the book, I will use this term to cover those in both co-parenting and sole parenting set-ups. I know every one of us will have a different arrangement and situation, and it is hard to encapsulate every one. So, I can only speak from my perspective and from the women who I have interviewed. And I hope some of the milestones and experiences I have gone through will be helpful and will add to all the brilliant and brave journeys that are already out there.

Having spent the last year reading hundreds of single-parent stories, I found each one helped me, gave me encouragement to keep going and provided me a window into a world of unbridled strength and love. I know that I have been incredibly privileged to live with my kids five days a week, and stay in my home, and I never take that for granted. But I want to share both the highs and lows of this new life that, although I didn't choose, I absolutely adore.

Technically, I became a single parent the day my husband left our family home. It became immediately apparent that getting ALL the jobs done in the home was now just down to me. In reality, I did a lot of it anyway, but there was no escaping it now. The bins, the broken drawer, the leaky shower, the kids' vomit, and the blocked downstairs loo . . . they were all mine to tackle. And they were now going to be tackled my way, and with no one telling me I was doing it wrong, either.

In the early days, taking on *everything* just felt unfair, shitty and tiring. I resented that I was left to literally mop up the mess he left behind. I remember one particular low moment was when I was home alone and defrosting the freezer. I was down on my hands and knees with a load of soaking towels around me, holding a hairdryer in one hand and butter knife in the other and I just lost it and yelled out, 'OHHHHH . . . FUCK YOU!' I really recommend this; it does help the defrosting process. Nothing melts away the thick ice like the fiery hot rage of an angry woman. What I wouldn't recommend, on reflection, is my somewhat questionable hairdryer/knife defrosting approach.

When the decision to become single is forced upon you, there is an overwhelming desire to just sit in a pile of bitterness. Sure, hang out with those feelings for a bit, but after a while – like the compost bin on the kitchen bench that you have chosen to ignore – it does start to stink. And do you know what is even better than having a good old tantrum about emptying the cat litter tray? Feeling like you are the BOSS OF FUCKING EVERYTHING. Finding the joy in conquering your home almost feels like you're winning a battle. I know there is such a thing as revenge porn, but I reckon revenge cleaning, decluttering or painting is even sexier. It's probably just as sweaty and sticky, but luckily it doesn't require you to shave your bush.

Strangely enough, I have discovered in this year of rebuilding myself and my life, it is the things that were the scariest and hardest that have become the things I am most proud of. No, I don't skip around the house feeling blessed that I am yet again the person who has to dispose of the sludgy half a cucumber at the back of the fridge, or the one who has remember to buy shitting dishwater salt, but when I assembled a firepit (screwed in three bolts), and we toasted marshmallows on it, I felt primal and fierce.

As a result of seeing their mother do everything and achieve things on her own, my children have consequently seen a side of me they hadn't before. A much more resilient and stronger side. And they often spontaneously recognise and praise me, by saying things like: 'you're doing a great job, Mum!'; and 'thank you for being the best mummy.' I am not saying it is perfect – Jesus, it is far from it; they also yell at me for giving them the wrong cup at dinner time, or scream in my face when I say there's only five minutes left of time on the Xbox – but the bond we have is so much stronger.

They have had to step up, too. Housework, especially during lockdown when it just seemed endless, needed to be shared among us. At the beginning, I know I spoiled them because I felt so guilty that their lives had been changed so dramatically. I allowed far more TV dinners, and endless snacks and treats. I wanted to make everything feel like a holiday. But, ultimately, that doesn't do them any favours long term.

When I look back to when I was married and the constant niggles about whose turn it was to do things around the house, I now get a strong feminist shudder. While being in a relationship is about compromise, and sharing the jobs, actually the workload felt bigger. Because along with the physical tasks, there were the larger tasks of dealing with expectations and disappointment. And I am sure he felt that, too; I will be the first to say I am terrible at housework. But, in many ways, having to do everything now means it gets done when and how I want it done. Sure, it's all a bit haphazard, but there's no let-down, no criticism or step-by-step instructions on how to iron a shirt. Fucking bliss.

Sophie Heawood, feature writer for the *Guardian* and author of the fabulous *The Hungover Games,* told me, 'I think that the energy people in frustrated relationships expend on resenting the other person is actually more tiring than just doing everything yourself. When I had a baby on my own, she cried in the night and I jumped up, she cried and I jumped up, and repeat to fade. Friends with husbands seemed to lie there in fury, waiting to see if he would actually get up this time, if he was really asleep, if he was pretending, if his body didn't respond to the crying child, if he didn't love them, if he didn't care. It all sounded exhausting, to be honest. I just got up and did it and then went back to bed. Of course I was shattered but looking at the washing-up in the sink didn't make me hate anyone. It was just washing-up in the sink.' And this is the freedom that single parenthood feels like, that there still might be shit to do, but it is shit without the resentment.

While I adore my new life now, one of the hardest hurdles in becoming a single parent was telling my children we had separated. Those with babies, or those going it alone from the beginning, have the freedom to pick and choose when they're told the stories. But, when your kids are older, this can be a very painful experience. For some children, it can be a relief that their parents are going to be apart, but for some it is a shock and very upsetting. Once the decision has been made for you or your partner to move out, then there's the issue of who gets the children and on what days. For some, their other halves may disappear and not see the children at all. Others split 50/50 and some need a degree in mathematics to decipher the intricate equations of percentages to work out that they go to their dad's place on every second Tuesday, but only when there's a full moon and there's a three in the date!

When the day came when we had to tell the children, we both agreed on what we would and should say to them. It was about two weeks after we had decided to separate, and he was living in and out of hotels and it was getting too difficult to maintain. We had read up on the language we should use and how we should do it. It was a strange moment of calm among the hurt and anger. It was almost easier having a focus that was away from us. We both love our children so much and knew that this was something we couldn't fuck up or take lightly. We set the table up and I put out a huge bowl of Skittles; I think these were more for me than the kids. It was all so odd; we watched them in the lounge, laughing at the TV, knowing that we were just about to change their lives. Every part of me wanted to scream, 'I DON'T WANT TO DO THIS TO YOU. I DIDN'T DO ANYTHING WRONG. THIS IS ALL HIS FAULT. YOUR DADDY HAS HURT ME AND I DIDN'T DESERVE IT. AND NOW YOU ARE GOING TO GET HURT TOO. THIS IS FUCKED.' But I didn't, and I wouldn't, and most people would NEVER do this, but that doesn't mean they don't think it or feel it.

This moment in all our lives wasn't about trying to decipher the fairness of it, or point to whose fault it was; this was about what was best for the two humans we loved more than anything else. This was the situation we were in, and we all now had to face it, and get through it as best we could.

When we were ready, we all sat down together. Both kids plunged their hands into the bowl of sweets and looked delighted. We explained to them that we loved them very much, but sadly we were separating. We told them that they would live with Mummy and stay in their home and that Daddy would find a new house that they would stay in some of the time. We all had a cry and took lots of big deep breaths. The kids were surprised, to say the least, and didn't understand why it was happening and they kept asking for a reason. We explained that Daddy had made some mistakes and that there were consequences. The kids asked, 'but why doesn't Daddy just say sorry?' I mean, they had a point, didn't they? Isn't that what we had always told them. Isn't that how it works? Daddy would say sorry, and then Mummy would forgive him. No, sadly, not this time. Mummy would not forgive this mistake.

Since speaking publicly about becoming a single parent, I am often asked by people, what is the best way to tell your children. As I have had only one experience of doing this, I contacted leading psychotherapist Philippa Perry, as she has written and broadcast extensively about parent–child relationships and is author of The Book You Wish Your Parents Had Read (and Your Children Will be Glad That You Did).

I asked Philippa, 'Is there a perfect way to tell your children you are separating?'

'Now, OK,' she replied, 'this is very interesting to me. We tend to think about our children as different species; like, you wouldn't ask me, "What's the best way I can tell Ellie about my divorce?" So think of your children as the two separate individual people that they are; you know them better than I know them, and you will know how to talk to them better than I can talk to them. I would not prescribe the best way of telling your kid about your divorce. I think you should tell them together because one wouldn't like to be intimate with you and the other one not. That would feel very weird. God knows it's hard enough telling your parents let alone your kids. I'm not saying it's easy, I'm saying that "Daddy isn't going to live here any more" . . . there's no sugar-coating that, "and you will probably miss him, and I am really sorry; this must be a bit traumatic for you."

'What is important to remember is, it's not something you tell your kids once. It's something they will need a lot of time to process and talk about. So it's not like we're having THE conversation and we never have it again, so it's like, "your mum or your dad isn't going to live here any more, we're getting a divorce, I think you might find it a big change," and then "how are you feeling about it today?", and then "how are you feeling about it all today?" and "what's the worst thing about it? What's the best thing about it?", and so on. You know . . . just that the conversation is always open.'

Philippa's wise words struck home very closely. My children and I have spoken about the divorce frequently since it happened, and I have always let them speak for as long as they like and need to. When we told them initially, it was so painful and hard, but they coped, and they got to stay in their own home for most of the time, so that changes were gradual and easy. But in that first month, one question kept being asked by both of my children: 'But why? Why did Daddy leave, and what mistake did he make? There must be a reason, Mummy?'

I could see this was troubling them both, so I sought advice from both my own therapist and our couples therapist, and we sat them down a second time and explained the reasons and that there are consequences to these actions. It was enough information for them to understand and it felt so much better not to have any more lies or secrets in the house.

I explained to Philippa what I had done, and why that had been the right thing to do for our family and children.

Philippa replied, 'It made sense for you to do that. If you don't give a reason, children will make up their own reason and, as a psychotherapist of adults, I often had, "I thought it was my fault, I thought Dad was leaving me," because they were kept in the dark. Secrets are not great. They can take, "Your dad likes dressing up in ladies' clothes" . . . "Oh, does he? OK, fine." They can take anything because your set-up is their whole life, so whatever happens in your home is normal to them, so even something that you think shouldn't happen, say, like, "Daddy isn't going to live here any more," is normal to them because it's all they know. I think the thing is not "how do I tell my kids"; the question is "do I keep talking to my kids about it and seeing where they are?" The main thing to tell your children is, "This is what it is, and we will have feelings about it, and we have the capacity to be happy whether we're two parents or one parent at a time."'

Giving your children the time to talk about divorce is so important. I spoke to the actor Tanya Moodie about her relationship with her daughter following her separation.

'My whole thing with my daughter,' Tanya told me, 'is that I think it's really important to be honest and to allow them the space to feel their feels. I just tried to let her come to me with it, rather than saying to her, "I think we should talk about this now"; do you know what I mean? And at one point, we were walking into school, and she said to me, "I'm really sad about you and Daddy breaking up," and I said, "You know what, I'm sad too." She was like five or six, still young, and she said, "What? You're sad!?" And she basically said, "Then what's the point, if you're sad? Why did you break up with him?"

'And I said to her, "Well, the thing is, if I stayed with Daddy, I'd be sad, but I'd also feel like I was gonna be sad forever, but now that we've broken up, I'm sad now, but one day I know I'm going to be happy and that's the difference." And then she was like: *Oh, OK.* And that was maybe the last time we talked about it. There was light at the end of the shit tunnel.'

Having these moments to chat openly with your children is really important. One of the things that made a huge impact on my children talking about their feelings was getting a pet. It provided quiet time together, and also another member of the house to cuddle. On the day we told the kids we were separating, I promised them that I'd buy them a kitten. Is it a coincidence that my ex is allergic to cats? This cheered them up so much. So Daddy was going to move out and we would be getting a cat. And a few months later we did, and then a few months after that, we got another, because we loved the first one so much. I think we will stop at two, probably. Cats are the best therapy.

My brilliant daughter took charge of the whole operation; she has been an animal lover practically since birth. We spent ages looking at kittens online, and reading books about looking after cats. We prepared for their arrival like a new baby was coming. Fozzie, who is now an enormous big fat black cat, arrived in June and Tigger, his little ginger brother, arrived four months later. As well as being absolutely cute and cuddly, they provided therapy and comfort to the kids. I noticed whenever either of the kids were feeling down, they would go and pick up a cat and would immediately be calmer. The cats would sleep next to the kids at night, and were often the thing they would first hug when they got in from school. We bought them Christmas outfits and spoiled them with treats and toys. I have never been a cat person, but these two fur babies brought our family endless love, as well as a couple of surprise dead 'gift' mice. Lucky us.

While I kept trying to build this new version of our family, I had to try to build a working relationship with my ex. Even though I despised him for everything he had done, he loved the children, and the children loved him back. And at no stage was I tempted to slag him off in front of the children, and we both tried our best to be civil to each other around the kids. However hard it was for me, the love I have for my children overrode any desire to get back at him.

I asked Philippa, 'Why is it so important we speak positively about our exes in front of our children?'

She cleverly replied, 'How do you feel when you hear someone you love being slagged off by someone you love?'

'Just awful,' I said.

'Exactly, you're split in two. I love them, and I love them, but they're slagging each other off. The other thing is I'm half Mummy, I'm half Daddy. If Daddy's really bad then half of me is really bad, especially if I'm a boy. If Mummy's really bad then half of me is really bad, especially if I'm a girl. So, I think you should have a nice little arrangement with your partner, a little agreement that you'll always talk each other up rather than down.'

But what happens when one parent starts to speak negatively or even make up lies about the other one?

Philippa explained that this is called 'parent alienation'. She said this is, 'when one parent is alienated from the child by what the other parent says. It's basically one parent poisoning the other parent to the child. It's like, "Dad can't keep it in his pants" ... that's poison; "Dad's got a new girlfriend' ... that's not poison. If there's a little vicious twinge to it, it's not great. When you're toxic or poisonous about the other person, and you might think that they are vile ... just cool the fuck down. It's not easy not to be toxic sometimes ... I think you can say, "I couldn't tolerate living with Dad's shoutyness; he shouts too much for me." Not say, "he's a maniac" but instead, "it's OK if you like shouting but I don't and the shouting got too much for me so I left Dad." Can you see the difference?'

Victoria Benson from the Gingerbread charity echoes this advice too: 'We tell people to always put the children first, and try to put all animosity to one side. But if you are in an abusive or difficult break-up, protecting yourself is also important. Arguing in front of the children will always make you feel worse, so make sure you have boundaries in place. If you feel like slagging off your ex, save it up and contact a friend. Find someone who doesn't mind you letting off steam. You will get the satisfaction of doing this, but not all the negative stuff you would get from shouting at your ex.'

Sharing your frustrations as a single parent, as well as your wins, is important. When I started talking about being a single parent on social media and on podcasts in June 2020, I didn't intend to have any agenda about what 'version' or 'tone' I was going to take. Mainly out of laziness, but it was just about sharing things as and when they happened. I wanted to highlight the experience of this new phase of parenthood, like I had done for the previous seven years of the Scummy Mummies. I wanted to honestly represent my daily ups and downs and my take on this calamitous journey, and yes, sometimes it's overwhelming, sometimes you're covered in shit, but for the most part it is bloody wonderful. I posted photos of the three of us cuddled up in my bed watching films and eating sweets, and many images of being happy about having my weekends to myself (with wine), but also just pictures of me looking enormously proud of myself for getting through another day. I wasn't slagging him off, or bitter; I was relishing in this new life I had been given, and wanted to shout about just how bloody good I felt about it.

What surprised me was just how many women started to thank me for representing them, and the life that they were living. I have received thousands of comments, messages and emails from fellow single mums telling me how much happier they were, and how much they cherish these moments of strength and connection with their children. I quickly realised that single parents were underrepresented and misrepresented in the media as a whole, but particularly positive and happy images. It is so ingrained in us to apologise or downplay our joy and independence as women. It's that classic trick of patriarchy that we have to always find something to criticise, like when somebody compliments you on looking good, and you say stuff like: 'Oh, this dress is really cheap'; or 'It's just because I'm wearing make-up!'. Why do we do this to ourselves? So, I felt a strong sense of responsibility and pride that I could use the platform that Ellie and I had built up over the years to give real and honest visibility to this parenting experience. I felt buoyed by this community of mothers that were championing me, but also for the mothers who were in relationships, who could get a window into what life was like 'on the other side'.

Social media can be an absolute torrent of bile, but it can be an amazing pool of support and has a vital role in shifting perceptions and understanding of single mothers and women. What I have discovered is that the community of women is incredibly supportive and is keen to show the realities of single motherhood, which involves so much happiness, independence and resilience. But it is also an important place to recognise the hardships and realities that so many single parents face.

I spoke with Ruth Talbot, founder of Single Parent Rights campaign, about the work she had been doing. Ruth runs the Instagram account @ellamental_mama and we discussed the importance of sharing all our stories. In March 2021, she released the Single Parent Discrimination Research Report, which surveyed over 1,000 single parents. Ruth told me, 'I've been a single parent for almost seven years and in that time I've seen and heard so many stories of discrimination. In Covid times, the impact on single parents was so clearly being overlooked by policymakers, employers and businesses, I decided to conduct a survey into single-parent discrimination, which found 80 per cent of single parents face some form of discrimination just for being a single parent.

'Many people don't realise, but the Equality Act outlaws discrimination against someone who is married or in a civil partnership, but it doesn't outlaw discrimination for single parents. Without a foundation of equality, single parents will continue to be discriminated against. This is why I've set up Single Parent Rights to campaign to change this and we are calling on the government to add single parents to the Equality Act.'

The report also revealed that '80 per cent of single-parent respondents experienced discrimination with 96 per cent experiencing or identifying its existence. Prejudice, institutional bias, and a lack of legal protections has resulted in an environment marked by distrust and disrespect for single parents, creating second-class citizens. Single parents living with a disability, from a BAME background, young and/or on a lower income, experience greater levels of discrimination.' The entire report made for sobering reading. And it gave me a much broader understanding of what sort of difficulties single parents face, from employment, housing and education to professional and social situations. And that we all, coupled people included, have a part to play in changing the attitudes to and opportunities for single parents and their children.

Through podcasts, blogs and traditional media, there are waves being made to change these outdated ideas. @singlemotheredit's Rebecca Cox frequently writes about the positives and realities of single parenting. Rebecca told me, 'the narrative around single mums is always, "Can single mums cope? How do they do it? How do they survive?", and it's never, they're having a great time, or it's like they're having a great time, in spite of the fact that they're a single mum. The story should be actually as a woman you can be really happy on your own, and you should know that you should be OK; you don't have to be with somebody else to be fine, and to be better than fine, to be fantastic. And if you hear women saying and doing that, then you will start to believe that. You don't need to have two people to raise a kid.'

Rebecca added, 'In my single mum group of friends, there's a really broad spectrum of different backgrounds, living situations, jobs, financial situations, and we all feel exactly the same. At the end of the day, most of us have got exes that we have trouble talking to (on any level) to arrange anything,

GET DIVORCED, BE HAPPY

and it's a shared experience. Everyone feels the same about society. One of the main things holding single parents back is the stigmatisation and how people still have this real negative view of the phrase "single mum", particularly mums more than single dads.'

I also spoke to the brilliant Khalifa Araba, who is the host of the *Happy Single MOM* podcast and has been a single parent for over ten years. Khalifa told me, 'I do think that society is shifting in regards to tolerance, but we still have a long way to go, even within our single-mother community. Storytelling is the key to helping people overcome, as they get strengthened by your story and mistakes. If not for the positive stories of other mothers, I wouldn't be where I am today as a single mother.'

And it is not as if single parenting is niche or uncommon. As Victoria Benson, the CEO of the single-parent charity Gingerbread, told me, 'There are around two million single parents in the UK, as many as one in three families are a single-parent family at one stage, so it is much more widespread than you would think.' So, our voices need to be louder and our stories need to be told.

Sharing positive stories about single parenting is, for many, hard to do, because it can also come with a lot of guilt. Telling the world that you are enjoying time away from your children, and that you're perfectly happy alone, goes against all those outdated societal norms of what is expected of you as a mother and what a family should look like. I spoke with the poet Hollie McNish about how she has found it difficult to speak openly about how much she enjoys her new life as a single parent.

Hollie said, 'For an average of two days every week I live totally and utterly alone. My child is at her dad's, safe and happy and loved. I am at home doing whatever I want (after work). To say that these two days are a joy is not an exaggeration; I love them. I can have anyone over, or sit and stuff myself with cheese and chips all night; I can have last-minute sleepovers at friends' houses after chatting till later than expected; I can masturbate for three hours; I can read a book or chat on the phone or stare at a wall. Perhaps best of all, there is nobody observing me doing any of these things; no judgement; no points deducted or scored. I am not responsible for anyone (a huge freedom as a parent). I do not have to ask permission or accommodate anyone else's timetable or mood or desires.

'I can leave my house with no discussions about why or where, or if anything's wrong, or how long I'll be. No, nothing's wrong, I just happen to fancy driving to the burger van at midnight and then watching films till 5am. And no one knows. And no one cares. In terms of mothering, for me, it undoubtedly makes me a much more patient mum, having time away from mothering. I also think it makes my child appreciate me more, but we'll see if that lasts. Saying all of this, admitting this happiness or positivity in time alone every week has been one of the hardest things for me to do; to other people; even, sometimes, to myself. Like I love it! Shhhh, don't say that. But I do!

'Of course there are positives about people who live and love together, but those are widely celebrated every day, while single parenting or co-parenting is most often held up as failure or "broken". But so often I find myself in groups of married mum friends especially, who are desperately lamenting former identities but made to feel too guilty to ask for some time away, as if they were not people before being parents and partners; as if to desire stepping from these two roles occasionally were some sort of rejection of either their partners or their kids. And in those moments, once again, I stay silent, because, well, I think they're right. It is fucking great to be alone sometimes. And I get it to do it twice a week. And then I feel guilty all over again for that happiness.'

Staying in a difficult relationship 'because of the kids' and not wanting to hurt them is an enormous barrier for women to leave. But, often, staying for their sake is so much worse for everyone. Victoria Benson said to me, 'I think we all know that two happy separated parents is better than being in the middle of two unhappy ones. We did some research two years ago and looked at the outcomes of children of single parents, and it confirms that. The worst thing that can happen to a child is to be raised in poverty, and that could be anybody. We all worry that we are damaging our children by becoming divorced or separated, but we are not.'

Changing this age-old doctrine that a 'happy' or a 'proper' family can only look like two parents and kids all together in one house has to change. The Aussie feminist and author Clementine Ford is doing incredible work to help women see that there is a life outside of this narrative: 'What I keep saying to women is, "I know we all want the best for our children; we want them to have the best food, the best state education, the happiest and healthiest childhood. So, why don't we think about our kids having the best mum?" And the best mum is one that is happy, that is respected, a mum that feels free and liberated in her life. Instead, so many women will put up, and endure, and will be downtrodden and will be disrespected in their own homes. I often ask women, "Would you be happy for your daughter to end up with a husband like yours, and would you be happy for your son to treat a woman like he does?" By changing this focus and having both respect for you and your children, it can only lead to better things.'

But, as I know, it IS daunting and scary, and unlike having a baby, there is no equivalent of antenatal or NCT classes for single mums. A lot of us don't have any time to prepare for it, or know what to do. But there is now a huge number of support groups, online networks and thousands of parents out there who will get you through this. Two of the best places in the UK are Gingerbread, which has a fantastic resource-packed website, online forum and helpline, and the Frolo app for single parents, which is an excellent place to meet fellow single parents and connect and share. However, essentially, like with most aspects of parenthood, most of the time you just get thrown in the deep end, and work out how to swim through the shit.

Working out what is best for your family unit is important. I spoke with Penny Wincer, the journalist and author of *Tender: The Imperfect Art of Caring.* Penny told me, 'When our children were just five and three, after eleven years of marriage, my ex-husband and I decided to separate. What made our situation complex was partly that I'm Australian and have no family in this country (my mother also died long before I had children) and partly because my eldest, Arthur, is autistic and has learning difficulties.

'When I looked at our little family unit that was not functioning as it should, I decided to prioritise what I valued most. It was more important that the children were in a home that was filled with love and connection and emotional security than whether or not I would ever be able to take my children to swimming lessons or birthday parties on my own, or even fulfil all my son's therapy needs.

'When the time came, my ex-husband moved out and we began our new arrangement of him coming to stay with the children every other weekend at the family home. I would leave the house and stay with friends while he took over. This arrangement worked well for our son, who struggled with changes and transitions. It also worked really well for our daughter, who was very young at the time, and always staying in her home, whether it was Mummy or Daddy who was there with her, was incredibly positive.

'With the help of tax credits, I hired a part-time nanny, the only childcare that was suitable for my son's needs. This has not been straightforward. In six years, we have gone through four nannies. From maternity leave and extended sick leave to quitting because it was just too challenging, keeping hold of childcare has been the biggest challenge for me as a single parent. But ensuring I have enough support to earn a living, as well as the support I need simply to function as a single parent with a child that has high needs, has been my number-one priority. It's not about scraping by with the minimum possible. It's about having what I need to sustain my own well-being. I know I can't be a good mother unless I feel supported, and, without family nearby, that has always meant paying for support.'

Victoria from Gingerbread told me, 'In the beginning you just don't know how you are going to cope without them on birthdays and Christmas. How am I going to share them? How can I have a holiday on my own? But you do cope with it, you do more than that, and you look forward to it.'

The first birthday we experienced as a new family was my son's ninth birthday in June. To be honest, it was one of the easiest birthdays I have ever had to do. We all got up together, and I made his favourite breakfast of bacon and pancakes, and then, after lunch, we had cake with a few mates in the garden and a mountain of sweets! All legal and distanced. By 4pm I was exhausted, at which point my ex arrived and collected both kids. Then I went on to have a couple of friends over in the front garden to polish off the chocolate cake, drink some fizz and celebrate my son's birthday! IT WAS HEAVEN!

My daughter's birthday in October was the opposite arrangement; she was going to be staying with her dad the night before and then we were to have lunch all together at the pub down the road. As a four. With him. I knew I was going to feel sick during the whole thing, but she wanted a family lunch together, so, even though it was hard, I would of course do this for her. It would be one hour of feeling uncomfortable; I could do this.

The night before her big day, I set up the balloons and stacked the presents like I always did. The house was so silent, and I knew it would be in the morning too, so I put on Irene Cara's 'Out Here on My Own' on repeat, and then I had the biggest cry. I hadn't cried for weeks, and it all just came flooding out. Waking up on your baby's birthday to an empty house is HARD. The physical absence of your child and missing the sounds of them jumping out of bed with excitement feels unbearable. But I knew she was happy, and that I would see her later on. So to get through it I just kept myself busy, rang friends, drank too much coffee and went for a walk. Like with so many of these firsts, I just got through it one step at a time, and I know it will be easier next year.

In our parenting agreement, we had decided to split the school holidays in half, which meant we both had six weeks each with the kids over the course of the year. Which also meant we both had six to ourselves; BRING IT ON! Single parenting is a lot like becoming a teacher in many ways, because the holiday perks can be bloody amazing (and very much earned!). Holidaying alone with my kids wasn't a completely new thing, because I had been a freelancer and stay-at-home mum for most of my kids' lives; I had spent many weeks with my kids while he worked during the summer or over certain holidays. I had taken them away for three days on my own, on little mini-breaks, but the prospect of doing a few weeks away with them on my own was new territory.

For our first holiday together, I chose to spend a week in the Suffolk seaside town of Southwold. We had been there as a family of four a couple of times, and also with my parents when they were over from Australia. We had happy memories there, and I knew where to get the best fish and chips and ice cream and bacon sandwiches on the beach, so that's pretty much all the essentials covered. There was something comforting in all the familiarity of the place, but I also know it seems slightly odd to go back to a place that might sting with the past and him, but I wanted to reclaim it as ours and flood it with new memories.

I had all the usual worries of how I would manage, how I would cope keeping an eye on the two of them at the beach. What if one needed the loo, and would I be lonely at night? Would it feel weird just sitting in the pub with two kids? And how would I survive taking them on the train and getting about? I don't drive, you see, and this is a massive pain in the arse. I know, I know, I just need to do it and get my licence;

becoming single has really highlighted that gap in my skillset. But, in the meantime, I just had to fumble along with taxis, suitcases, and bribing the kids with sweets until we got there.

I had just enough money to rent a tiny little cottage only two streets back from the beach, and I made myself lower my expectations of keeping it clean, or attempting to have any rules at all, and threw away any hopes of going 'screen free' out the window. We spent every day at the beach, either swimming, or going off to the pier for arcade games or crabbing by the river. We replaced fruit or vegetables with those lollies that made our tongues blue and so many chips, and stayed up late every night. And what I kept noticing was that I felt so free just to be relaxed. I didn't have to worry about someone else's needs, or their fitness requirements, or how they liked their eggs cooked, or what time they thought the best time to swim was. And I felt like I was a child again, too.

What I thought was going to be stressful and hard work ended up being one of the most cheerful holidays we had ever had; it was a massive revelation and turning point in my recovery.

Saying that, getting away on a holiday as a single parent is not easy, logistically and financially. Having spoken to a range of parents about what they have done over the years, here is a list of some survival tips.

Holiday tips for single parents

- **Double the Fun, Half the Cost –** When planning a weekend away, or a week by the coast, book a cottage, caravan or camping site with another single-parent family or even organise a whole group of you. It makes getting away so much more affordable, and that way you have an extra pair of hands on deck, playmates for your kids and you might even get ten minutes' rest to yourself.

- **House swap –** A cost-effective way to have a holiday is to organise a house swap with another family. Even if it is just down the road or in a neighbouring town. And there are plenty of websites through which you can sort this, such as the *Guardian*'s Home Exchange and Love Home Swap.

- **Borrow some gear –** Don't be afraid to ask to borrow a friend's tent, or beach gear, or any summer holiday stuff. Chances are they won't be using it, and will be happy to help.

- **Screens are your friend –** Don't feel guilty if your kids watch a bit more telly, or play an extra game of *Mario Kart,* when you're on holiday. If you need them to keep busy while you're packing the suitcases at the last minute, so be it. Just be kind to yourself.

- **Don't pack too much extra stuff –** Getting your things from home to holiday, even if it is in the back of a car, is exhausting. It doesn't matter if your kids wear the same pair of shorts two days in a row – nobody ever died from wearing a slightly dirty T-shirt. Lower your cleanliness expectations and have a day off from domestic duties.

- **Keep it simple –** It's tempting to try to do lots of activities, but especially in the early days of single/co-parenting, just getting through three meals and maybe a walk to the beach or the shops to get an ice lolly is enough.

- **Your kids just want you –** Life is frantic and sometimes overwhelming when you're the only adult, so allow yourself to throw out the rule book and be a big kid too. Your kids want to spend some time with you, as well as playing video games and watching YouTube videos of cats.

- **It will be different –** Travelling with kids alone is a big task, but also incredibly fulfilling and packed with opportunities to make new memories.

- **You are not alone –** There are lots of fellow single parents out there to give you tips and advice about holidays and getting away. Mumsnet, Gingerbread and Frolo are a great place to start. Ask any question, and you are sure to get some friendly advice from those who have years of experience and expertise.

While we'd had numerous wonderful holidays together as a family of four, and those happy memories will stay forever with the children, it is hard not to look back on many of them without a sharp twinge of pain. It is heartbreaking knowing that when I thought I was being loved and sharing a life with someone, they were also sharing part of themselves with someone else. I know in time I will have more peace with it, but it is difficult not to feel that those happy times weren't enough, or that they weren't overshadowed by somebody else. So, it now feels exciting that every trip away and mini-break with my children in the future will be just ours to curate, to cherish and feel proud of. And maybe next time we might even eat some salad, but I doubt it.

Our first Christmas as a new family came at the same time as another national lockdown, so that chance to share it with more than the three of us wasn't even a possibility, but in many ways this was what we needed. Like with the birthdays, we went with what the kids wanted, and what we both could cope with. And, like birthdays, there were too many presents and just us stumbling through. The kids were away for the week before Christmas, so, for the first time, I had all their presents out and just wrapped them whenever I liked. That felt relaxing and easy and the prospect of only cooking for three was incredibly appealing. I asked them what they wanted and of course they replied, 'pizza'. I suggested we all just choose three things each, and two of them had to be vaguely healthy. So, on the day, we had macaroni cheese, pizza, roast chicken and cucumber, cherry tomatoes and carrot sticks and all the Quality Street we could eat. So Christmassy!

On Christmas morning my ex came over to do presents and hang out in the house for an hour. It was of course the first Christmas we wouldn't spend together in twenty-two years. It was so strange for it to be just so chilled out and calm. So many other years were stress fests, with us shouting at each other about when to put the potatoes on, or making sure the meat wasn't overcooked or driving off to family in a panic. We had lots of happy times, of course, but this was the first time I just didn't have a constant list in my head of what he was doing or not doing, and letting that go made me feel lighter, and just better.

When he arrived, I stayed in the house for two minutes to watch the kids enthusiastically show him the presents they had got from Santa and then popped over to a neighbour's garden and drank Buck's fizz. Again, like holidays and birthdays, it was surprisingly relaxed because I had lowered my expectations and just enjoyed the day. The kids were happy, I was happy, and lockdown seemed like a blessing, as there was no rushing off anywhere.

And I was spoilt too. On Christmas Eve, Ellie surprised me and popped over with a bag of presents, just for me. It was a stocking filled with wrapped gifts from her and a whole bunch of friends; it was one of the kindest and most thoughtful things I have ever received. (She would like it to be known that this was a one-off.) I laid them all out under the tree and basked in the huge wave of love. There were little things, like my favourite Aussie biscuits, cocktails, nail polish and special treats.

Also, the week before, I had taken the kids to our local gift shop and given them my debit card and worded up the woman who worked there. I told the kids to buy me a few things and get them wrapped up, so I had something nice underneath the tree. I highly recommend this, or even get a friend or family member to take your kids shopping. I know presents aren't everything, but I am not going to lie and say I don't like getting pampered occasionally. I ended up with a candle and a pair of dangly earrings, which were surprisingly lovely and sweet. Honestly, it was the best Christmas haul I have ever had.

What surprised me was that I didn't feel the absence of a partner, but more the presence of an overwhelming amount of love. I mean, there was a point at around 9pm when I did really fancy a good snog from a hunky man, but I think that was the Baileys talking, and I knew that could wait. And, of course, the best part of the day was that I didn't even have to leave my own house.

I know this year will be my turn to give them over, so I asked my friend, YouTuber and author, Louise Pentland, for advice, as she's had a few more years' experience.

'It's hard not having your offspring on Christmas Day,' she told me. 'I miss my daughter every other year. BUT I remind myself that she's actually OK, she doesn't feel my sadness, she just feels Dad joy and fun and is making memories with her other parent, which is healthy. I read a thing that said, "Don't let your storm get your children wet". So, on Christmas Eve, I'll say, "You go and have the BEST Christmas ever and I'll see you on Boxing Day!!" I tell her that my heart knows when she's having fun and that makes me even happier so that she doesn't feel that weird attachment guilt thing either. It helps to know she's good and happy. Then you can just go and have a big wobble into a trifle and be a good parent.'

While I got through the big milestones OK, one of the toughest things I have had to face is that of my children meeting my ex's new partner. A few months after we separated, he met someone else and started a new relationship. During the summer, the kids began to tell me that Daddy had a new friend; it had barely been six months since he had moved out when I was told that the kids would be meeting this new woman.

I remember it was during the period I was on a three-week cleanse from alcohol, wheat, dairy and FUCKING COFFEE, so I was feeling very raw and fragile when he called to tell me this news himself. I was lying on the sofa, shaking, as he spoke. I tried not to cry as I took it all in, and just kept it together. I felt so protective and so frightened. It wasn't that I was jealous, or even cared that he had another partner; it was just that I didn't want the kids to get hurt. It felt too soon, and too weird for this all to be happening. But I had to trust that he would look after them and that they would be safe. I was at home alone, and I would have usually just run to the closest bottle of wine or gin and necked it, but instead I just lay down, sobbing really loudly, and sank into the sadness of it.

I knew that this day would come, but it happened before I was ready and before I had healed. It also brought home how much I wanted the divorce to be formally processed. We were still technically married, and he was now in another relationship; was it easy for him to just forget what I had given him and the years I had spent loving him? Did that even matter? That was the hardest part, but also so useful in moving forward for myself. There was no more love to be found from the past, and, as much as I wanted what I had given him to be cherished, acknowledged and respected, it was time to let that go.

In terms of introducing new partners, Philippa Perry told me that, 'I think if there's too many new partners it's not great, so, if you've got a new boyfriend or girlfriend each weekend, I don't think that's terrific. Children don't need that. They can meet different friends obviously but if they're "Special Friends" then I think wait till the relationship's established, steady and likely to go on indefinitely before you introduce children, because they get attached to the new person, and they have another bereavement when the new person goes again, so that isn't great, as then they feel "I've been left again".'

My single parenting friends have all told me that they have waited at least six months into a relationship, if not more, before they introduced a new partner, as they just wanted to make sure that this person was serious. My children were really happy for their dad and liked his new girlfriend, so were naturally curious about when I might meet someone and start a new relationship. I know this may happen, but honestly, and as I keep telling them, my time with them is their time, and I like that my dating life is separate and just for me. And since I am determined to meet lots of different people before I go anywhere near a new relationship, it isn't something I see happening for quite some time. My friends have become my significant others and I am more than happy to keep it that way.

The only new relationships I am keen to develop are those with other single parents. But I know it isn't always easy to find them when you're in a sea of married couples. Zoe Desmond, the founder of the Frolo app, told me this was the reason that drove her to create this platform. 'The idea for Frolo came from wanting to know where people were locally; did they have kids the same age. It has made such a difference to my life. Just having my closest friends I have met through Frolo, who live around the corner. They are like extended family. And I have lots of friends I have made through the app. My son, Billy, gets to hang out with other single-parent families and not feel different, not left out. So he is growing up feeling like there is nothing wrong with my family and going between two homes.

'That is the power of having a community of single parents and having other people there to support you, like share the funny stories of dating, or empathise when you've been up all night with a sick kid and there's no one there to help with that and share the burden. It is so special to have other people who get it. Non-single friends and family will lend support, of course. But there is an extra understanding when people are in the same boat.'

Victoria Benson, from Gingerbread, echoed this. 'One of the best and most helpful things for people is hearing from someone else who has gone through it just before you. Because they can provide you with reassurance. When you are constantly around married and couple friends, you can feel like you're being judged and that remains a challenge for single parents, and they can feel isolated.'

Over this past year, I am grateful that I now have a new network of single parenting friends who help me through the tough times, and are there to cheer me on through the milestones. There are still days when I feel overwhelmed by all the jobs, and there is nothing more exhausting than trying to balance childcare, work, that washing mountain, and making sure you have a papier mâché Stonehenge ready and painted for Wednesday morning. And yes, on so many levels it is more work, I have less money, and the negotiations and administration have been heavy going, but as a mother I feel stronger, more focused and have more energy for both them and myself. I now feel so ashamed I ever entertained the thought that I wouldn't or couldn't love being a single parent, because it has been one of the happiest and rewarding things to happen to me. And, to be brutally honest, it has given me almost the same amount of joy as the arrival of my two precious babies. It *has* been like another birth, but this time my fanny stayed intact and I didn't have to breastfeed anyone, thank God. I absolutely adore being on my own with my children; I just wish I had someone who had told me just how wonderful it could be. So I am glad to get to tell you, and the whole fucking world, about it.

Things I have learnt about being a single parent

- You are not alone! When you become a single parent, you unlock a whole new community of parents who look out for each other, whether that is online or in your neighbourhood. Don't be afraid to seek out new single friends and share your experience with people who understand what you're going through.

- You don't have to be brave all the time. Ask for help when you're struggling, or don't know how to do something. No one expects you to instantly be an expert at everything, and some days are just hard. Gingerbread, Mumsnet and Frolo all have online places where you can get in touch with other parents to help you out with advice on anything from budgeting to dating again.

- Having the freedom to create your own home, your own spaces and how you spend your time with your kids is powerful and rewarding. Creating a new family unit and building new traditions together is a wonderful opportunity to bond with your children.

- Some days it's hard to hang out with married couples, and it's OK not to go to events if you don't feel up to it. There are no prizes for feeling miserable. Do things when you feel strong and ready for them.

- Don't sweat the small stuff and learn to let go of having a clean house. Life will probably be more chaotic, the washing piles a little higher and kitchen sink a little fuller, so be kind to yourself – the kids don't care if there isn't a clean surface in the house, and neither should you.

- There is no shame in being a single parent. In fact, it is the opposite of that; you should be incredibly proud of yourself and what you achieve on your own. If people make you feel bad for being on your own, that is entirely their prejudice and nothing to do with you.

- If you get some time on your own, enjoy it, and try not to feel any guilt about wanting to have a good time and feel happy. Use this free time to do things just for you, whether that's having a bath or taking up a new hobby. I know this takes time, and of course you will miss them, but if you are able to get some days off, revel in this time and freedom.

- Always be nice about the other parent in front of your children. Your kids don't need to hear what you really think of your ex. Even if you don't have a good relationship with them, always hold your tongue, and just be polite about them.

6

My Support Crew and the Strength of Female Friendship

How do you put into words what your friends and family mean to you? How can you say thank you to the people who have been your comforters, your warriors, your tea makers, your wine pourers and your shoulders to cry on for an entire year? It's impossible. I have sat down so many times, and tried to articulate the strength, compassion and kindness that I have received from my dearest ones, but nothing quite cuts it.

It is almost animalistic what I feel for them; it's like it's in my bones and nervous system. I would tackle a bear, or punch a shark, or even try to calm down an overtired sugar-fuelled toddler for them. My divorce has given me many wonderful things: freedom, a new outlook on life, time to myself, and, yes, a whole drawer full of new sexy polyester pants. However, the most important gift has been realising just how fucking amazing my support crew is and the strong circle of love that surrounds me. You are all the fizz in my Prosecco, the mayonnaise on my chips, the snort in my laughter and the wiggle in my hips.

I have been incredibly lucky that, from the very first moment my husband left, I was nestled in the bosom of some almighty badass bitches. But I also know that this isn't everyone's story or experience. I understand that for many people separation is lonely and isolating, or they choose to go through it alone. For me, I count every person who has helped me as an absolute godsend in my hour (and year) of need. And I can only tell my own truth. My separation has been, at times, public and I have welcomed the help and advice, and I want to share what I have learnt from it.

At the beginning, when I was very much in shock, my friends rallied around and spent days and days just listening to me grieve and rage, or sent me flowers and gifts to cheer me up. One day my neighbour Claire spontaneously arrived with a takeaway coffee topped up with Tia Maria. Those who had been through divorce were especially good at just knowing what to do.

Just a few days after I found out, my friend Hollie picked me up in her car on the Sunday morning, bought me some Vogue menthols and walked me around Dulwich Woods. She had gone through divorce three years prior, and she filled me with comforting words and minty fags. She reassured me that, yes, it was totally shit, and would be for a bit, but then everything was going to get better, a lot better. And that was exactly what I needed; just to know that this pain was going to go away one day.

The endless gestures, generosity and time that were given to me was extraordinary. What was most valuable during that time was not only the gifts of doorstep lasagne, but just how emotionally available my friends were for me whenever I needed them. However, the lasagne was also very helpful!

As I mentioned before, I did these first few hard months in total lockdown; I did all of it with the absence of hugs, pubs and leaving my house. So phone calls and Zooms were the closest things I had to human connection. My best mate Taryn in Australia called me every day at 10am, and told me I could pick up or just leave it, but she would just always be there. This was wonderful, and I highly recommend this to other friends supporting your mate going through this. What was also wonderful was that friends who I had always just texted began to call too. My dear friend Rose would call late at night, and always started the conversation with, 'Darling, how are you?', in the most loving voice. All these interventions of kindness kept me going, and kept me from sinking.

That said, I wasn't used to being the one who was being looked after. I have always wanted to be the friend who brings the cake, organises the birthday hampers, and who never fails to have a spare bottle of Cava for playdates. Having to just sit and be metaphorically held and not give anything back was uncomfortable, but I had to let go of what I thought I *should* be for friends, and accept what I *needed* from them to survive this colossal head fuck.

My three wise women from Australia – Ceinwen, Shannon-Kate and Taryn – were incredible. As I mentioned, they were the first people I told when my marriage ended, and have lived through every high and low of this year, on every single day. They were there at university at the beginning of my relationship with my ex, and now they were here for me at the end, except via WhatsApp rather than a pub in Melbourne. And what was hard was, they had loved him, too; in fact, two of them were his friends before I even met him. I call them my wise women because they are a trio of geniuses. There's a whip-smart lawyer, a steely financial whiz and a kindly librarian who has already gone through divorce. They are everything to me.

Shannon-Kate wrote to me and said, 'To be honest I did not know what to do or what to say. I could only speak in the most natural way, and tell you my heart was breaking for you. What made you an incredible friend for all of us through this period was that the first thing you did was ask for help. Second guess or figure out how you were feeling, we could not. Many a drunken night I'm sure I dished out unsolicited advice, and you took it graciously. The time difference between Australia and the UK was a godsend too, and as a group we galvanised.'

So I had my late-night advice helpline sorted. And then there was the amazing Ellie for almost everything else.

Our friendship goes beyond anything I have ever experienced in my life. Ellie has taught me so much in these past eight years: everything from how to stand up for myself, to how to cook the best spaghetti carbonara, to what 'tea-bagging' is (don't google it). While Ellie and I have been in a double act as comedians, and loved dicking about on stage together and writing sketches, one of the reasons I think we have been mildly successful and why women tell us that they value what we do is because we talk about our female friendship in all its messy glory.

Look, I'm not saying we are inventing anything new, and it largely involves us sharing pictures of us at boozy lunches and being massive idiots, but that imagery of us as best mates and the bond we have resonates strongly with so many. While we may not have equality yet, women are by far the superior sex when it comes to friendship.

So, when I had to break the news to her that my marriage was over, I knew this would hurt her. But she didn't know about it for a whole week: I couldn't tell her as she was in Japan with her parents on an amazing holiday. They had planned this trip for years and I could see she was having a wonderful time. She was sharing joyous moments and photos and I knew that it would ruin it for her. I deeply wanted her wise words, her humour, her amazing hugs, but I had to hold on. She only had a few days left of holiday and I had a whole lifetime of being divorced. It could wait. But those days were long. We later joked about how, by holding back my news, I saved her from making her holiday really shit – what a gift I gave her. You're welcome, Ellie.

On the morning she returned to the UK, I texted her first thing:

'Hey dude, give me a call when you get this message.'

A few long minutes later my phone rang, it was time to tell her, which went like this:

'Hey dude, what's up?' she said; she had such a happy voice . . .

'Hey man, Japan looked amazing. Umm . . . Ellie, I am really sorry.'

'Shit dude, what's happened? Are the kids OK?'

'No, they're fine . . . It's over. He's left and it's awful.' And then I did a cry that could only be described as bovine. You know those sounds you heard on *All Creatures Great and Small* when James Herriot has half an arm up the back end of a cow.

'Fuck, don't go anywhere. I'm coming over. I am getting in the car *RIGHT NOW*.'

I blinked and she was outside my house. I went to the front door and we embraced. There she was. My friend, just there, just holding me. We sat at my kitchen table, she made me tea and I told her everything. And then she went to get me another cup of tea, and, when she got to the sink, she broke down and cried. I could see her body collapse. My strong Ellie was broken. And then I went to her and we sobbed together, and she said, 'I'm so sorry this has happened to you, dude!' Yes, we call each other dude, a lot.

Ellie will be the first to say that she doesn't 'do' emotions. She's the funniest, smartest and most sarcastic person on the planet. She doesn't do soppy or sentimentality, but she has the biggest kindest heart I have ever known. To see her so sad was hard. Usually when she gets teary about anything, she quickly says, 'Oh, there's something in my eye!' That morning, after we had a good old ugly cry, she said, 'You're gonna be all right. It's shit, but we are going to get you through this.' And with her as my wingwoman, how could I not be all right?

Throughout the whole year, Ellie has done little daily acts of kindness, like spontaneously making me lamb biryani, or organising a surprise Zoom with a group of friends when she knew I was really down, and was just always at the end of the phone when I needed to be angry or cry. But the most spectacular thing she did was for my birthday. She spent weeks putting together a massive scrapbook of photos and messages from all my friends and family, and a few fabulous podcast guests, too. It was called 'The A to Z of Helen' and she handed it to me at my birthday lunch. I remember her saying, 'look, just LOOK, at how many people love you, Helen; you don't need a man!' And she was right. I was encircled with extraordinary people who poured buckets of the good stuff all over me. I wouldn't wish what I had gone through on anyone, but what I am grateful for is to see the true love that I always had around me in a new illuminating light.

My ex wasn't devoid of kindness, and I did receive many gifts and cards from him through the years, but I remember one birthday, a few years before our separation, where he wrote in a card: 'Here are the five reasons I love you' – a strong start, but then below that he only wrote two things, because he told me he couldn't think of any more than that.

OK, hold on, there are two things wrong here: one is the fact he wrote it; and the second is that he gave it to me like that. Why would you do that? What was he thinking? I laugh about it now, but it did symbolise how my marriage and relationship felt, that there were bits missing, that I wasn't enough for him.

So, in contrast, to have an entire book with hundreds of reasons why I was loved brought home how rich my life was. Again, I know I am incredibly lucky here. He was just one person, a person who I didn't need in my life any more and certainly any more birthday cards from.

While I know not everyone can make a book of love for their mate, I do believe that there should be a gift registry for freshly single women, just like a bridal registry. There needs to be a kit of new, gorgeous and practical things. Here's what I think we should give our single-parent mates.

Single-Person Survival Kit

- **A New Duvet Cover –** It is strange, but there's something magical about having new bedding. If you have to keep the same bed, make it feel different and jolly.

- **A Badass Sharp Knife –** Nothing like chopping up carrots, aubergines and chorizo with vigour to help with the healing process!

- **House Plants –** Having greenery around you has been proven to improve your well-being, so surround yourself with lots of luscious plants.

- **A Drill –** This is essential. There is nothing better than screwing in a bolt or just holding a drill and giving it a few pulses to make you feel like Wonder Woman.

- **A Skip –** Get a bunch of friends together and hire a skip for the freshly single person. And then have a chuck-out party. Even if you just buy a whole lot of plates from the charity shop and smash them into it, it will be worth it.

- **Photo Frames –** Print off lots of gorgeous photos of you, your kids and your friends and put them all over the house. Surround yourself with love.

- **Sex Toys –** A good vibrator is the gift that keeps on giving. Just don't leave it in the shower like I did, and have your cleaner discover it.

- **A Day with a Gardener** – If they have a garden, buy them some new plants and hire a preferably hot man or woman, so that they can sort your bush out.

- **Red Shoes –** There is special power within a sexy pair of red shoes. Even if you can't walk in them. They are a thing of beauty.

But, ultimately, your single mates just need to know they are loved.

Sharing these moments of brokenness and sadness has not only been therapeutic and cathartic for me but it has allowed many friends to open up about their relationships, or previous periods of darkness. They've told me about their parents' divorce, or times when they faced betrayal and lies, and we have sat together over a few drinks, and been vulnerable, open and just that good kind of pissed. So, by doing this, we have become rock solid. The women in my life give endless love and time to each other, and rarely ask for anything in return, and nothing is being brushed under the carpet any more.

As the author Kathy Lette told me, 'husbands come and go but girlfriends last forever. I think women are each other's human wonder bras – uplifting, supportive and making each other look bigger and better. I would be totally flat without my female friends. I'm lucky enough to have three warm, wise and witty sisters and many fabulous gal pals. When we get together, we have to be hospitalised from hilarity, but we also strip off to our emotional underwear in a psychological strip tease that reveals all. You know how that always happens at a girls' gathering? We're all laughing and joking and, then suddenly, we're all hugging and crying? But we always end up guffawing again by the end of the night and, more often than not, in the bar, swinging from the chandelier with a toy boy between our teeth. Sounds about right, doesn't it?

'By the way, do you know why it's called a "wonder bra"? Because when you take it off, you wonder where the hell your tits went. My advice is to never wonder where your girlfriends have gone – keep them close. Cherish your female friends, mums, sisters, daughters – let your cups runneth over with love. Let this be your femifesto – to stand on your own two stilettos. Don't wait to be rescued by a knight in shining Armani; let every man know that you no longer want his seat on the bus – you want his seat on the board – and keep your human wonder bras buoyant.'

When it comes to friends, I realise I'm speaking from a very heteronormative perspective, as a straight woman. And I know my experience of friendship and separation is not the same for everyone, even though there will be common ground among what we all experience.

When I spoke to Rosie Wilby, the author of *The Breakup Monologues*, she told me about some of her experiences as a gay woman going through separation: 'As a lesbian, you can sometimes fall into the trap of your partner being everything, with them being your best friend and your lover, and it all gets wrapped up into one thing. Straight women friends have generally done better at separating and having a group of best girlie mates. My girlfriend at each point in my life has been everything. I have lived a very intense type of monogamy, which has translated into a rapid cycle of serial monogamy that's been fuelled by this intensity of relationships. And interestingly, lesbians are the group where divorce is at the highest rate, as women can really throw themselves into relationships quite quickly.'

Part of me was slightly jealous of the type of relationship that Rosie had described, about having that intensity and being everything to someone and them to you. It sounds wildly romantic and all-encompassing. It made me think about how I had wanted that sort of relationship, and how I'd thought that was what marriage was going to be like: best friends AND lovers ... dreamy. The longer my relationship went on, the less I wanted that. And it was often my friends who I wanted to have the long dinners at fancy restaurants, or weekends away, with. Why is it that when your friend eats noisily, you find it a billion times less annoying than your husband? I know I am not alone in thinking that I would rather spend time with my friends than a grumpy partner; frankly, they are more fun, and I don't need to give anyone a blow job at the end of it. Win-win.

One of the other things I discussed with Rosie was what she describes as a 'hierarchy of heartbreak'. Rosie told me that often members of the LGBTQI community receive less sympathy when it comes to break-ups, and that somehow their heartbreak is considered less significant than those in straight married relationships with children. And this needs to change. While I had had a pretty shit separation involving infidelity, I will be the first to say it certainly didn't mean the pain I felt was any greater or worse than someone who had been in a relationship half the time, without kids or with someone from the same sex. Pain is not an Olympic sport or something we can put a number value on. And we all would like a cuddle and a lasagne, please.

The way that we separate has an impact on how people can perceive we are coping or how much support we need. I spoke to my friend Natalie Lee, who had a much different break-up to me. She told me, 'I am not very good at asking for help, first of all, and also I feel like because it was me that made the decision to leave the marriage, people have kind of expected me to be OK and I haven't had an outpouring of "come here and let me cuddle you, give me a big hug" kind of thing. Because I've got that kind of strong capable persona as well and I'm crap at asking for help so people have been like, "Oh, she's fine," especially when they look at what I post on social media. They're like, "Oh, no, she's absolutely fine, she doesn't need anything from us." That's been quite annoying, I must admit. I have had some words, especially with my family, like, "I'm also finding this fucking hard. I'm having a hard day too."'

Support from family can also be incredibly important. I have a big family of Thorns that are not only connected to me by blood, but also the type of people who you would want to get pissed with, eat kebabs and drunk dance to Bananarama with. I mean, they annoy the shit out of me, a lot of the time, but when there is a crisis, they are at their best. I also have four extraordinary sisters-in-law who have each piled me with endless support, but the most important family member is my big sister, Claire. She's eleven years older than me, and has been a best friend and a second mother to me.

She also understood exactly what I was going through. Twenty years ago, I woke up one Sunday morning to a phone call from her. She told me that her husband had just left. For her, it also came out of nowhere, and her life instantly changed. That morning I hopped in a taxi straight away and was with her within half an hour, and pretty much didn't leave her side for a year. I moved in, stayed up many nights smoking and drinking, holding her, drying her tears, and just getting through it day by day, beside her. I remember thinking how angry I was with her ex for hurting her deeply and how I would have given my legs to see her happy again. Part of me wonders if having lived through this experience is one of the subconscious reasons that made me try to hold on to my marriage so hard. It is interesting that, instead of it putting me off marriage, I was determined to make mine last . . . not knowing that the decision of staying together wasn't going to be mine to make in the end.

Remembering what I went through with Claire made me realise that it is what she and my friends were doing for me now. To me she never felt like a burden because I cared for her so deeply and just wanted her to know she was loved.

Because of the pandemic, I still haven't seen my sister, or my parents, in a year, which is heartbreaking; but, despite being on the other side of the world, Claire was on the phone every day, and still is. Thank you, darling sister, for being so patient, making me laugh, as well as consoling me. And sorry if you heard the same stories on repeat. I hope you know just how much I love you; you're my everything.

In the first few days after separation, having a sister or someone you can just be totally yourself with is crucial as well as having someone to be honest with you.

Samantha Baines, comedian and host of *The Divorce Club* podcast, told me, 'My sister came to stay with me at the beginning and for three days I just sort of sat with a swollen face from all the crying, and stared into the distance for quite a long time, didn't change my clothes and didn't wash. My sister was staying in my bed with me, because I didn't want to be on my own. I had this fear of it and then I think around day three she was like, "Erm, I really think you need a shower, because you stink," and that's what sisters are for.'

I acknowledge that I'm greedy and love having a whole smorgasbord of people in my life that I can nibble or gorge on at any one time. I am also fortunate that I didn't lose many friends because of the divorce either. Depending on the circumstances of your separation, friendships can be tested and, sometimes, sadly lost. Divorce can bring up tensions in relationships, and in families too. So, your network of support may look different, and that is OK. But the good news is you will also get new friends. 'What, are you insane?' Trust me on this one.

I know this seems like a ridiculous prospect, when you can barely reply to some of your best friends. However, when I became single, it unlocked a whole new group of women for me, like a secret level on a video game. I became part of a brilliant group of humans who are the survivors and thrivers of divorce, and they are impressive – and they wanted to help me! Women who have experienced affairs, betrayal, the break down of a relationship or just a shitty partner, became mentors through this.

Also, during this time, there will be friends who can't cope with what you are going through, and won't know what to say. While this might be hard when you are relying on someone close to you for support, it may just be too tricky for them. Psychologist Dr Rachel Masters said to me, 'Sometimes friends will react in ways you are not expecting. Maybe it is that they are in a difficult relationship and your separation is triggering for them, and they don't want to hear about it.

Remember, your separation can be incredibly confronting for them.' So try not to take it personally. Some of them will return when they are ready, but, in the meantime, you will find friends who can be there for you.

WARNING: There might be some women who will be weird about you being near their partners (urgh! As if?). Fuck them. Well, fuck them off as friends, and don't fuck their partners, obvs.

When I spoke with Rachel she said to me, 'We need to set up the equivalent of AA for newly separated people. Everyone needs a sponsor to get them through those first few years. And tell you things like, "Yes, it's OK that you are going through your slut phase right now. That's what you are meant to do." This is exactly what you need; you need to know what you are feeling is COMPLETELY NORMAL. And you will go through many phases.'

As much as friends in long-term relationships were there for me, it was vital that I found a small group of people who understood exactly how I felt. Especially when it came to my 'slut phase' and dating again. It's funny how many coupled-up friends aren't as interested in your new sex life as you are. I found this out the hard way. Sorry friends, you really didn't need to have a blow-by-blow-job report after every date night, did you?

Surprisingly, another thing I found incredibly heartening were my male friends who just picked up the phone and offered words of love and support, or just listened and said, 'I'm so sorry, mate.' It was an old university friend, Steve, who is in fact an actual man and has known me and my ex-husband for over twenty years, who provided me with one of the most uplifting sentences. He said to me, 'Helen, the good news is that every day you get to wake up as you, and he has to wake up as him.' I have repeated these words over in my head hundreds of times. And he was right.

Telling my broader circle of friends was another hurdle that, although difficult, was – for me – part of the process of accepting this new life I had. I didn't want old school mates and work colleagues finding out via a public podcast or random Instagram post, so I decided to do a private Facebook post. I know these can be cheesy, but there was something quite liberating about just being 'out there'. This isn't for everyone, I understand. I drafted a few sentences and sent it to my ex for approval. Even though things had been difficult between us, I wanted to be respectful. I wanted to just let everyone know the kids and I were happy and that we were now a content team of three. Which, was, of course, the truth.

I posted it on the Saturday morning and then, all of sudden, my phone exploded. Outbursts of concern and wise words came flooding in. I felt overwhelmed by kindness and compassion. This was in mid-June, after three months of just surviving and bumbling through. I now felt I was coming out of the fog, but then I had that urge to reply to everyone, especially when old friends started private messaging asking 'what happened? I thought you two were always meant to be together?' or 'please call me, I want to hear everything'. I spent the day just recounting bits and pieces of the story, picking and choosing who I told what. By the evening, I had made myself feel sick with it all once more.

I was alone in the house, and felt even more alone, even though I had messages of love. Telling the story of the end of my marriage now feels much easier, and sometimes I even laugh or add in a joke. But this just takes time, lots of time.

Dr Rachel Master told me, 'There is an element of not wanting to put too much on one friend. It is really important to have different friends for different reasons. I have a couple of friends who know everything about my sex life; I have a specific WhatsApp group just for that. And then I have my divorced friends who are really practical and are great at telling me "not to take any more shit!", and these are the ones who got me through my divorce and really got me through the shit . . . the real "go-getter" friends. And then there are the emotional-pillow friends, the ones you can fall into tears with at eleven pm and just sob on the phone with.'

So with that in mind, here are some suggestions about the type of friends that are useful during the throes of a break-up – and, I would argue, for life! Obviously, friends can take multiple roles etc, etc, etc – make your own rules – or, if you are happy by yourself, all power to you.

Here are some of my suggestions . . .

THE SPORTY FRIEND

Find a mate who you can regularly exercise with. It might just be a walk to the supermarket to buy more fags, or a stroll around the block while you have a cry, but get a buddy who MAKES YOU LEAVE YOUR FUCKING HOUSE. Chances are you are wearing leggings already and you have a pair of trainers knocking about, so move your sad arse a bit. Another great thing about becoming single is trying something new (no, I am not talking about anal). I mean, this is a brilliant time to discover, and try, different sports. I know cold swimming is basically the new ecstasy among the forty-plus brigade, but I found things like weight lifting, Pilates, yoga, tennis – and even some terrible paddleboarding once – strangely uplifting and helpful. Anything to do with your body moving is bloody fabulous. And if you have one of those bossy but encouraging friends to push you a bit, that's even better. I know it is all of the clichés, but exercise will make you feel better and you can still shout at your friend, 'THEY WERE SUCH A CUNT TO ME!', when you're out for a nice bicycle ride around the park.

THE BOOZY FRIEND (OR CAKEY ONE)

If you're anything like me, most of your friendships will be based on how much you enjoy sinking a few pints of Pinot Grigio with them. Alcohol isn't always the answer, but having someone you can have a bit of a silly blowout with occasionally is really important. If you don't drink, find a mate and indulge in something you both like. Like cake, or cheese, or whatever takes your fancy – well, apart from crack and heroin . . . stay away from drugs, kids. I had a few excellent mates who I knew I could rock up to their places with a few bottles and chances are we would get through them and then polish off that dusty bottle of Cointreau at the end of the night. We would laugh, I would probably cry a bit (lot), we would dance to the Pet Shop Boys and order a late-night kebab. And there was no judgement if you had to do a quick little lady vomit on the way home. All part of the healing process, really.

THE CUDDLY ONE

Everyone needs a friend like this; when they aren't even holding you, just their presence feels like a warm hug. These are the friends who have probably known you for a long time; you could probably both sit on a sofa playing Candy Crush or reading some shit novel and neither of you would care. They are also the ones who say things like, 'No, you're not fine. Tell me how you are really feeling?' They know where the tea is in your house, and they just start folding your clothes or sweeping your floor, and it is lovely, rather than judgy, like when your mother-in-law does it. If this friend was a Spice Girl, she would be Baby Spice. Also, this is not compulsory, but it does help if this friend has a good rack; there is something lovely about getting a hug from someone with fabulous breasts.

THE GLAMOROUS FRIEND

I am not saying you need to be friends with Joan Collins, but wouldn't that be great? And I'm sure she has excellent advice on divorce. Just find someone who you essentially play dress-up with, even if it's over an oven pizza and a tub of taramasalata. I have a few friends that make me up my game when it comes to frocking up and looking presentable. I know it's shallow, but I love a friend who makes you want to put on your best clothes and feel a bit fabulous. When you are feeling low, sometimes dragging an eyeliner across a lid or squeezing into that push-up bra you got on sale from ASOS is a good thing, not for anything other than feeling delicious in your own skin.

THE GET SHIT DONE FRIEND

Righto, this is a friend that you REALLY actually need. The one that sits you down and says to you, 'What do you mean, you don't have a bloody pension?' And makes sure you start getting the right advice for your divorce. I know many of you (me included) avoid anything involving numbers, forms, and hard things like having a ten-year plan. But I have been blessed with friends who are accountants, lawyers and clever clogs, and they don't want you to get fucked over. And neither do you. Don't be scared by the sheer amount of paperwork that is involved in separation. YOU CAN DO THIS. And don't be embarrassed to ask for help. There are friends who literally get hard over Excel spreadsheets. Just go with it. And for God's sake, be honest about how shit you are with money. Now is the time to pull up your big girl pants and learn about compound interest. Yes, it's boring, but it is a feminist act to be good with your cash. Do it.

THE ANGRY FRIEND

As mentioned earlier, Ellie was magnificent at channelling my anger and rage. It was like I had outsourced it to her. Also, you might already be excellent at getting angry, so you may not need any further help in this department. However, I found, as someone who shies away from conflict, having a few friends that can get angry and have that brilliant female rage energy is really wonderful. You know, the type of people who say things like, 'That's bullshit, you don't have to put up with that!' or 'You've got to be fucking kidding me! No, that's completely unreasonable.' Swearing is obviously vitally important, too, especially when going through the meaty bits of separation. The great thing about having angry friends is that they act like your rocket blasters; they will propel you forward when you have run out of fuel and are just surviving on fumes.

140

THE SELF-OBSESSED FRIEND

Stay with me on this one. Some days what you need is to be distracted from your thoughts and your sad face and just entertained by a friend who can talk for days and seldom asks how you are. I have a few friends who I ADORE WITH MY WHOLE HEART, who rarely ask me anything more than, 'You're OK, right?', and I really like it. Sometimes it might be that they want to fill the silence and don't want to say the wrong thing about your situation, or others are just so excited about telling you about how smart their son or cat is, or that they are having problems with a leaky boiler. Sometimes just someone banging on about their own problems is a good way of getting you out of your own hole.

Beyond my friendship circle, I have thousands of women supporting me through the work of Scummy Mummies. If you have listened to a podcast, followed us on Instagram or been to one of our shows, please don't underestimate how wonderful you are, and how much your support has meant.

One of the most significant things we did in this past year was record the podcast announcing my separation. It is one of the only episodes we have released without a guest – just the two of us. The other was a really raw and moving one, just three weeks after Ellie's son Joe was born prematurely back in 2014. Baby Joe was still in the hospital and Ellie was there pumping her boobs, and preparing bottles to take back to him. We sat together and let the words and tears flow, as well as the breast milk. It was extraordinary that Ellie could even speak; she was, and is, incredibly strong.

This podcast was also incredibly special, because we did it side by side, in the same room. In June 2020, the government allowed single-parent families to 'bubble' with another family, which meant I could go to her actual house and HUG HER for the first time! Suddenly getting divorced felt totally worth it.

For anyone who experienced lockdown alone, you will know that absolute relief of what that first hug from a loved one felt like. OH MY GOD, the exquisite joy of finally being fully embraced. Sure, I'd had the kids cuddle and climb all over for me for months, but it's not the same as a big all-encompassing body smash. Ellie and I are huggers. It's not only just part of our day-to-day life together, but it's part of our show ritual and professional life. At every show we have done, just before we go on stage, when we are waiting in the wings and hearing the buzz of the audience in the theatre, we always have a big squeezy hug. I always pat her on the back, and we say stupid things to each other like, 'Tits and Teeth!', and then we are ready to leap out in front of hundreds of people. That first hug felt like that, like we were about to start a new chapter and brand-new show together.

So when we sat down to record this podcast about surviving the lockdown and the breakdown of my marriage, it was really about how our friendship got us through this insane time. We both spoke about how Ellie supported me and how I had to accept help. She spoke about how difficult it was at times to be the carer. Usually when we do our shows, I have prepared questions and a running order and we obviously have a guest to bounce off. But this time we just sat down and let the words and feelings flow. We both cried and made each other laugh, and said twatty things about banana bread and *Tiger King*, but it was raw and honest. I didn't mention how I became single, or any details about what had happened; it was more about how I was still managing to stand up and get through each day and rebuild myself.

When we released the podcast the following week, we had no idea about the impact it was going to have. We always get a few comments, or emails, for each episode, but nothing prepared us for what was to come. Within twenty-four hours, we'd received a huge number of comments and emails from around the world from women (and a few men) who had gone through separation and divorce, who were offering their love, advice and stories.

It was extraordinary. I was overwhelmed with the generosity, and, suddenly, this instant community of strong, fearless humans emerged. Some, who were children of single mothers, told me how much they loved and respected their mum for what she'd done for them. And others told me of how much they loved being by themselves. And of course, others wanted to tell me about what amazing sex I could soon expect. BRING IT ON.

The connection you can feel with strangers is remarkable. Showing our vulnerability, and how broken each of us were by what had happened to me, opened up a whole new group of strong women.

I kept thinking back to what my friend Nelly had said to me about my ex 'doing me a favour'. While the hurt was unbearable to begin with, as I started re-establishing myself as a single person, I felt I had a stronger sense of purpose. The marriage that I had so desperately wanted, onto which I'd clung to make me feel complete, was not what I needed any more. I felt more alive being single, and feeling the love of my friends and the power of the women who were championing this new stage of my life was the beginning of something even better than marriage.

Things I have learnt about friendship and accepting help

- It is OK to say you're not coping. There are no prizes for getting through a separation without help and being brave, when what you really need is a hug and a lasagne.

- Give friends specific tasks to do. They sadly can't read your mind, and will understand if you just need them to buy you three packets of Jaffa Cakes and a bottle of Villa Maria.

- When you're ready, open up about your feelings with those you trust. By sharing your pain, it may allow them to confide in you too. Being vulnerable with each other can bring you closer together.

- Don't feel you have to tell everyone the full story of your separation. And, if possible, get close friends or family to tell your broader circle if you want people to know; this way you don't have to manage the text messages and take on other people's reactions.

- You can't control how others will respond to your separation, so try not to take it too personally. Separation can be very confronting for individuals for many reasons, and this is not your fault.

- Having fellow single friends is really important; if you don't already have these, you can find welcoming communities online that will give you virtual hugs. I have found that the divorced/new single club is a supportive group.

- You are not alone. The path of recovering from heartbreak and separation is a well-worn one, and there will be someone to help you at every step of the way, whether that's those close to you or those you can connect with virtually.

Ellie's bit

I never believed in love at first sight. The first time I met the man I married, he was standing in a pungent halls of residence dorm room, wearing a scruffy tracksuit top, and holding an enormous contraption constructed out of an old bucket and a length of rubber tubing.

'This is the bong to end all bongs,' he told the assembled company. 'We call her . . . The Mother.' Weirdly, I did not immediately think, 'Ah yes, here's the father of my children.'

In fact, another six years and several boyfriends would pass before we got together. And even then it wasn't as if Cupid's arrow suddenly pierced my heart. I was just a bit pissed and thought he might be worth a punt.

The first time I saw Helen, I was stone-cold sober. It was my third-ever stand-up gig, and I was old enough to have learnt that, in fact, alcohol doesn't make you funnier. I was sitting in the audience, shivering nervously.

(I know most people sweat when they're nervous, but the 'comedy club' was actually a shipping container under a flyover in Deptford. There was no heating, and it was so cold they gave the audience blankets. Showbiz.)

The woman who walked on stage wasn't nervous. She didn't look it, anyway. She was bold and confident and gorgeous and hilarious. Within twenty seconds, she'd made me belly laugh twice. Within sixty, I was in love.

No, not the kind of love that makes you want to take off all your clothes and mash your private parts against theirs. But love comes in different forms, and many can be just as potent as the sexy one. Just ask anyone who's ever had a child, or a beloved pet, or a really great electric blanket.

What struck me most was that she just seemed to radiate this light. It shone out of her, illuminating the room with such power you could almost forget you were in a shipping container in Deptford, trying not to think about what that blanket smelled of. I was instantly drawn to it. (The light, not the blanket, which I later burned.)

No, I did not look at her and think, 'I want to start a hit podcast with this woman, become her double-act partner, set up a business, write a moderately successful book together, build a social media following, and perform a sell-out comedy show to thousands of people all over the UK.'

I just thought, 'I want to be her friend.' And to this day, while all that other stuff is brilliant, I know our friendship is still the biggest prize of all.

The thing about loving someone, of course, is that when something bad happens to them, it can feel like it's happening to you too. When Helen's marriage ended, I knew that I couldn't really understand what she was going through. I would not pretend for a second that I know what it's like to experience the full force of that impact. But I did feel the shockwaves. They reverberated through my own life like a fart in a bath.

First came the shock. I could not process how anyone could do something so hurtful to this wonderful person I loved. No one deserves horrible things happening to them, not even horrible people. Well, maybe Laurence Fox.

But I couldn't understand how anyone could do this to such a loving, kind person. I knew how much Helen had fought for this marriage, how much more of a giving, selfless person she was than, say, me. It just didn't seem fucking fair.

And that's where the rage kicked in. I'm a grown-up; I understand people fall in and out of love, and I don't believe anyone should feel forced to remain in a situation that makes them unhappy. But I also believe we should treat each other with respect, and take the kindest path even when it's the hardest. And if we make mistakes, I believe we should own them, and do our best to heal the wounds we've inflicted – or at least limit the damage.

Although I understood on an intellectual level that this wasn't happening to me, I did experience some of the same types of emotions as Helen – within a different context and to a different degree, of course, but nonetheless powerful.

I too felt betrayed by this man. I thought about the holidays we'd been on together, the laughs we'd shared. I threw away every jokey gift he'd ever given me, knowing that every time I looked at them I'd be reminded of him.

I remembered how, just a few months previously, I'd conspired with Helen's husband to arrange a surprise weekend away for them. It was my idea, and I did all the work, but I let him take the credit. I wanted her to have a decent Christmas present from him, for once. Now I wish I'd just bought her a really great electric blanket.

A few days after I found out, I went for a run along the Brighton seafront. I ran past the piers and right up onto the cliffs towards Saltdean, where the roar of the traffic competes with the crash of the waves. I screamed and yelled and shouted into the wind. I called him all the names. I told him exactly what I thought of him. It's a shame he wasn't there to hear it, but at least the seagulls got to learn some new swears.

At the end of it all, I was still angry, but the rage was no longer burning me up. It had become a galvanising source of energy, a white-hot furnace within, ready to forge whatever tools I would need to get Helen through this, and to keep our business going. It also turned out to be exactly the right temperature for cooking lasagne.

Just to be clear, though: I never doubted for one second that Helen *WOULD* make it through, either with or without my help. I knew it was going to be incredibly painful and difficult, but she is one of the strongest people I have ever met; for all her wonderful softness and kindness, she has a rock-hard core that will get her through anything.

I understood I couldn't fix this for her, no matter how much I wanted to, so I resolved just to be there, to help in whatever way I could, and to keep our business ticking over while she poured her energies into healing herself.

Which all sounds great, and having something to focus on definitely helped me, but, of course, there were days when it all seemed too heavy, or when I felt totally out of my depth. I learnt, as Helen did, to turn to others in these moments – her sister, our friends, my mum, that guy I met at university with the bong. They helped me carry the weight, and reminded me I didn't have to bear it all on my own. I will forever be grateful.

These have been hard times. I'm not sure there are many things worse than seeing someone you love in terrible pain, and feeling unable to make it all better. And yes, I am still angry.

But it has also been a privilege and a pleasure to watch Helen emerge from this and become who she is today. I wouldn't say she's changed, because she's still very much the woman I fell in love with in that shipping container. Instead she's now able to flourish and grow without restraint. Her light shines brighter than ever, because she is free.

I am so proud of all that Helen has accomplished. I am so happy to have her in my life. I know that this new chapter is going to be amazing for her, and I am so grateful I get to share it. I can't wait to see what adventures we have next.

7

Getting Shit Done! Get That Lawyer and Sort Your Money

Moving on and breaking myself away from my marriage took months of hard work, but I have discovered that all the therapy, exercise, heavy lifting, sexting, shagging and emotional growth in the world doesn't make you 'officially' divorced. And it was now time to face the music and get it bloody done.

I'm not going to lie, the legal process of separating and sorting out the finances scared the absolute shit out of me. And from speaking to many other women, confronting the paperwork, admin and the sheer expense of it all, not to mention having to interact with your ex, can be one of the biggest barriers to leaving partners in the first place. But, again, like childbirth, and learning how to fold a fitted sheet, you can do it. And there are so many people, YouTube videos and resources out there to help you smash it.

Finally getting divorced or officially separating from a long-term partnership can feel like one of the happiest days of your life. Along with you moving into separate homes and dividing up your treasures, getting that final piece of paper – that decree absolute – is a magnificent moment of official liberation and provides a genuine and seismic opportunity for closure and celebration. But getting to that point, as we all know, takes time, energy, money, an upheaval of your emotions and just so many goddamn emails and phone calls.

Whether you are married or not, I like to think the big finale is similar to the beginning. Because, like weddings or commitment ceremonies, there are so many different ways you can do it. It can be a simple affair, cheap and cheerful, involving just the two of you and some officials, or it can be really expensive, over-the-top, take months to prepare for and involve everyone (including Aunty Beryl) sticking her oar in where it's not wanted. Basically, it all comes down to how willing and agreeable both parties are about dividing everything up. You can choose to sit around the kitchen table and split everything in half over a cuppa and a Bourbon, or some choose to go through mediation; others, sadly, will need to spend time in court. This is the part of the breaking-up that isn't pretty – in fact it's pretty ugly – but, fuck, it's satisfying when you get through it (and I've run a long way in my pants, so I should know).

For me, personally, getting through the official bits of divorce essentially came down to three things: compromise; resilience; and having a support team around me – a legal team and a team made up of friends and family. Like with a marriage, divorce feels like one massive life lesson in compromise; it's rare to get absolutely everything you want, and even rarer to get through the process without having to negotiate and let some things go. When you are already in a fragile state, having to settle for less than what you think you deserve is a bitter pill to swallow. And yes, there were times when I felt like having a proper toddler tantrum and throwing my toys around, because the to-ing and fro-ing was so draining and maddening, and at times I thought I wasn't going to be able to cope. But I kept thinking that each little compromise would lead to decisions being made, and those decisions meant that I was ending my marriage and being able to move forward and on with my life, which meant that, in the end, it was going to be worth it.

Resilience is also key to surviving this arduous part of the process. There were so many times when I thought I would be beaten by the paperwork, or the ridiculously long mediation meetings (on Zoom at fucking 9am), or the thought that I might have to leave my beloved family home for good. But I had to keep going, keep fighting and keep defending myself. I can't count the times I picked up the phone to a friend and said, 'I just want this to be OVER!', as everything took so much longer than I'd expected or wanted it to. But then I'd do some deep breathing, have another coffee, phone another friend and just keep going.

Having a badass support crew was essential for me crossing the finishing line in one piece. My parents were there at the end of the phone when I needed a cry, and a virtual hug, and just kept saying 'we are so proud of you!', which, of course, made me cry even more. Ellie was brilliant (obvs) at getting really angry and being like a human power pack when I had run out of strength and energy. And my incredible sister, Claire, was like my motivational coach, always knowing the right thing to say, and always making me see the funny side to the ridiculous situation. And then, of course, there were the legal and financial brains that I needed to get the thing rubber stamped and completed.

My support crew were also important in getting me over the line. Obviously, you can do this alone, and all power to those who get through those forms by themselves. I am lucky that I had a few good friends and family to help hold my hand, but, that said, there are so many amazing resources online, as well as single-parent support groups, that can guide you through both the legal stuff and the best ways to separate.

I have many friends who have spent years being separated and who have not got around to processing their divorce, because they had a good working relationship and there was no hurry for them to go through with the dreaded fucking faff of it all. And other people I know couldn't get divorced because their ex refused to agree on anything. I, on the other hand, wanted to get divorced as quickly as possible and thankfully my ex agreed.

While I was dealing with the shock of it all, I also got legal advice within the first month of the break-up. I needed to know exactly what the hell was ahead of me. I spoke to divorced friends, listened to podcasts, and read extensively online about 'how to get what you want after a separation'. Because of the way my marriage ended, and the way my ex had behaved, I was determined that I was going to get 'justice' as I felt so angry (justifiably) that my future, my financial situation and the financial situation for our children, and the way I wanted to live my life and had expected to, had been shattered and destroyed in front of me.

I know this seems painfully obvious, but finding the right lawyer is really important, even if it's just to give that initial advice of what might be the best course of action for you and your particular situation. What is really brilliant now is that divorce is spoken about much more freely, and without shame and stigma, and you can find a lot of advice and support networks online and on social media.

Laura Naser, family lawyer and author of *The Family Lawyer's Guide to Separation and Divorce: How to Get What You Both Want*, runs an Instagram account called @thefamilylawyer where she provides excellent tips, advice and guidance to those of us who are going through it at all stages of the process. And one of the most important things that she advises is making sure that you get the right lawyer for *you*. How do we actually make sure that we do that?

Laura said, 'Finding the right lawyer can be really difficult; recommendations, if you can get them, are good – from friends, and also going on the Resolution website, www.resolution.org.uk, which is a community of family law professionals; we all sign up to this extra code of conduct to be amicable and put the children first. That's quite a good resource for finding a resolution family lawyer in your locality. You just put in your postcode and find lawyers that are close to you. Though in this day and age of Zoom, I of course now have clients everywhere. But it's a personality match really, and a huge part of what I do on Instagram, and somewhat also with my book, is about that, so people can watch me, see me, hear my voice, see how I communicate, and that I am an expert in my field, so that when people instruct me, they can then feel that they already know me. They have that connection and some trust in me.

'You need to feel comfortable telling your lawyer the worst things that have happened in your life; you know, the awful things going on behind closed doors that you may not tell your best friends, so you need to feel comfortable with them. You also need to be aligned in your values. You don't want a lawyer that is super amicable if you're saying, "Look, I've tried

everything and now I just need you to get this done for me."
You might, in that case, want someone more assertive. You've
got to do your research and pick up the phone. I spend a lot of
my time having that first chat with people because personality
does matter as well as expertise, and not all lawyers do all
types of family law, so make sure you marry up expertise
with the right level of experience. Your case should be handled
by someone with appropriate experience, depending on the
complexity of your disputes, and what the individual tasks
required to progress matters for you will involve.

'And don't always be led by cost. Don't choose someone
down the street because their hourly rate is lower than a
lawyer at a bigger and more renowned law firm; that someone
down the street might take twenty hours to do something that
the bigger firm can do more efficiently, as the firm can split
the job among a team, and some can then work at the higher
hourly rate on the complex parts, and some at the lower
rate – say a junior, supervised by the senior lawyer. That way,
the team can get it done in a time- and cost-efficient manner.
Hourly rates alone can be misleading.'

Laura suggests, 'There's no real "right time" to obtain
legal advice, but I would say the sooner the better, so that
you're better informed. People will say things that they've
once heard – in the pub, for example – and I talk in my book
about the dangers of friends and family; although they want
the best for you, they may not be telling you the right things.
What happened to your neighbour, best friend or aunty may
not happen to you and it may panic you. Then you've got the
"pub divorce lawyer". The "Google divorce lawyer" is also a
danger because you could be googling away and reading
something that relates to Scotland or America, where the laws

are different, and that may not be obvious from what you're reading. I think getting legal advice early on is key, when you're ready for it; doing it as soon as you can will start helping the process so you are informed of correct information and you don't start your discussions about separation on misconceptions, incorrect law, or misunderstandings.'

I asked Laura, once you have found the lawyer who is right for you, 'How long does it ACTUALLY take to get divorced?'

'Divorce itself,' she said, 'which is the legal dissolution of your marriage, is a fairly straightforward process, and it can be done via post or more commonly online. This in itself can take a matter of months. What people don't always appreciate is that running parallel to the divorce is the issue of separating your finances. Although separate, they are intertwined. This part is really down to how long it takes for you to provide the necessary financial disclosure, and then negotiate, and agree on, your financial separation. If you agree between you, or go through mediation, that can be quite quick, and if you can agree, you might do it in just a few sessions and then you're actually just waiting on the court to approve the paperwork for the divorce and financial agreement. But if you can't agree between you or in mediation, then you might need to try solicitors' negotiations, and that can take months if you don't agree. If you have to go to court, then that can take even longer. There are some other options, such as collaborative law and arbitration, which you could discuss with your lawyer to see whether they are suitable for you. The shortest time could be three to six months, but this is rare and tends to be held up by the court's backlog of admin, unless you need it with urgency, and then longest time, one or more years. It really comes down to how swiftly you can both reach an agreement, so that's even more reason to be amicable and reach a compromise.'

Finally, I asked Laura for any other helpful and juicy tips she would give someone starting to go through the process of divorce. And she wisely said, 'Be cautious about what you're posting on social media, both during the relationship and afterwards. There's a section in my book that's titled #*Blessed*, and it's got things like people posting on Father's Day: "He is the most amazing father in every way. Thank you for all you do for us . . ." And then, when they come to the separation and looking at the arrangements for their children, they might suddenly be saying, "You're not a very good father. You shouldn't have the kids 50/50." The father can then use the previous social media post to undermine that allegation, such as: "But when we were married, you were saying what a wonderful father I was" etc. So, be cautious about what you post, don't start going for the jugular and airing your dirty laundry on social media, slagging them off, getting into disputes with their relatives and their friends, because that can get really nasty.

'The other thing I say to my clients,' Laura continued, 'is change your passwords, because you know we've all got our phones synced with our iPads and our laptops, which are synced along with your emails, with your family computer, which they might have now taken, so things can pop up on that. And don't allow yourself to snoop; if you can see their messages popping up on the family iPad, don't look, because that's a breach of confidentiality and it's a breach of privilege if it's from their lawyer. And then it can get worse, and it can get criminal and the police can get involved. If you start sending nasty messages to your ex, calling them names etc, and they stay *Stop communicating with me* but you carry on anyway, that may become an arrestable offence and you could get a criminal record and all the ramifications that come with that, so proceed with caution.'

What Laura had told me – and what experience friends had with regards to getting legal advice early on and starting the process rather than putting off, or avoiding it – felt key. Also, as much as I was filled with rage and wanted to mudsling, it wasn't going to help me end the marriage, or help the kids, or get me where I ultimately wanted to go. I had a whole group of people I could bitch to over copious wine, and that was good enough. So it was time to take a deep breath and face those fucking forms.

Saying all of this, you *can* go through divorce without a lawyer. If you and your partner split amicably and are agreed on how you want to proceed, then getting through the official stuff is just a matter of paperwork. And it doesn't need to be expensive or time-consuming. But getting legal advice is really important if you want to absolutely make sure you are getting what you want and need.

I ended up choosing to use a lawyer, because I was such a mess emotionally, and I wanted that extra advice and guidance. A friend recommended a woman she had used; she thankfully wasn't expensive and I knew that she had been a calm and kind support.

I remember that first call to her. I was walking in the rain, and giving her the full rundown of everything my ex had done, and I just spewed out all my hurt, anger and disbelief – still, I realise now, in shock. She listened patiently, she was supportive when I said what a shit he had been, and provided a calm voice at the end of the phone. But then the punch in the guts came. She said something along the lines of, 'Helen, I know what he did to you was terrible, but none of this counts in the court of law. And if you do decide to go to court, then you'll probably just end up with fifty/fifty, straight down the middle, in terms of your assets.'

My shock was doubled. 'But, but, but,' I stammered, 'he did this, to us, to me – THIS ISN'T FAIR!'

The sense of fairness during a separation is contentious and heavily emotional. And it is still a very difficult thing for me to resolve, even though I have somehow managed to get through my divorce and have survived. Yes, I wanted someone to pat me on my head and say, 'Well done, Helen, you were very well behaved in your marriage, you didn't cheat, and you tried your best, so here's your divorce certificate, a badge and half a million pounds.' But it doesn't work like that, and it feels like that is still wildly sexist and patriarchal.

Having got the lowdown and initial advice from my lawyer, I decided to contact Sarah Langford, barrister and author of *Sunday Times* bestseller, *In Your Defence*, for her advice and to get a better understanding of how it all worked. Sarah had been a guest on *The Scummy Mummies Podcast* back in 2019 and I remember jokingly asking her for divorce advice a few years before, on behalf of the listeners who may be considering it . . . little did I know. What I do remember her saying very firmly is, 'Whatever you do, just try to stay out of court!', which I thought was hilarious coming from a barrister. So, when we sat down to chat, of course the first thing I asked her was, 'So OK, how *do* you stay the fuck out of court?'

'Find a way to bite your tongue,' she replied. 'Keep it clean. Wait for a day before you text or email anything and then go back and take out the bear-baiting bits. And keep telling yourself that no matter how much you want a judge to punish your ex, it is not a court of morals; it is a court of law. The law is interested only in a fair division of assets and what is in the best interests of your children: it is not interested in previous wrongs, or who has behaved badly, unless these have a bearing on who the children live and spend time with. Moral fairness is not always the same as legal fairness.

'What is really hard is when a woman has given up her whole life for a man, and it is usually that way around. She has left work, looked after the children, sometimes moved countries for him, been his PA, and sacrificed her own opportunities for someone who has fucked her over and THAT is very unfair. But the court is there to try and address financial fairness and is ultimately there to help decide what is best for the children.

'I always say the best thing to do is stay out of court; however, there are some cases where this is unavoidable. At every single turn, I try to tell clients and friends to ask themselves the question, "What am I gaining, and who is this for?", because often the answer is not as simple as, "because I am entitled to it and this is the right thing to do." Sometimes going to court is out of confusion or wanting to hurt, and sometimes it is complicated.'

I told Sarah, 'One of the things I kept thinking was, it wasn't my fault; why do I have to suffer, when I didn't do anything wrong? This feels like the hardest thing to rationalise within the framework of the law.'

'I hear you,' Sarah replied sympathetically. 'I've seen some total bastards at court, really nasty vindictive ones, and ones who have done all the classic betrayals. It's hugely unfair to have to give the one who cheated or behaved appallingly anything at all, and you just hope that their judgement day will come, not with a mortal judge but an immortal one.'

Now with some understanding of the reality of what court may look like, I was determined to stay away from it at all costs. Going to court is expensive and can take months and months (if not years), and I really couldn't afford that, nor did I want to draw this out any longer than it needed to be. My ex and I both wanted to be divorced and for it to be over with. As we were still just about able to be in the same room together, we decided to go ahead with the mediation process. This basically means that you sit down together with a very calm professional and lay out everything you have and everything you want, and then you keep talking, and going back and forth, until you can come to an agreement on who gets what, that both of you can live with. It's all done with a flip chart, a stack of coloured pens, boxes of tissues and two slightly angry people, trying to control their emotions and their tempers. That's how I saw it, anyway.

I found a local mediator, who had also previously been a lawyer, and she was everything you could want for such a difficult process; she was calm, softly spoken, looked like a kindly librarian and explained each step of the way clearly. While it was the best option for us and our situation, it was far from easy. Finding the strength to sit down with my ex to talk about the nitty gritty of it all was incredibly painful.

We began the meetings in the autumn of 2020, as I had just started to feel stronger, happier and at peace with my new life, so then having to spend two or three hours sitting next to him every fortnight was like opening a fresh wound each session. The first few sessions were in person and the final few were over Zoom (THANK FUCK, because at times I would just cover his infuriating face with a Post-it note on my screen).

While the process is incredibly confronting and fucking hard, I was surprised how empowered and strong I was during the negotiations. I felt I could speak my truth and articulate my wants and feelings without losing control or getting overly emotional AT LAST. But, sometimes, when discussions were difficult, I did look at him and feel heartbroken. A year before I would have done anything to make sure he was happy and for us to be happy as a couple, but now we were arguing over what percentage of the house we would both get. Even though I held on, after each session I felt numb and overwhelmed with both rage and sadness. It can be awful and I don't want to pass over this aspect lightly.

Deciding on who had the children when was, surprisingly, not a difficult process for us, and we went with what the children wanted, which was two days a week with their dad, plus half the school holidays. But these decisions aren't always easy, and are always able to move and change as the children grow older.

Laura says, 'When you separate with children, the court's priority is what is in the children's best interest. Older children may tell you what they want, but if you have quite small children, then their opinions won't have much weight, as they have little understanding of what is best for them.

'It has to be considered around practical arrangements, who can pick the children up from school or childcare and what works best for everyone. If one of you has to move further away because of housing, then that needs to be taken into account.

'The pandemic has really changed things, as people are working much more flexibly, so I have seen a lot more fifty/fifty child arrangements, because parents are able to work things out together around work rather than be dictated to by working hours. But it must always come down to the child's needs. If your child has additional needs, they must be addressed.

'Once you have agreed on your arrangements, it is not set in stone, because factors will change over time – things like the children getting older, and practical things like people moving, their activities, and what they want to do. Especially on weekends, when the children are older, they may want to spend more time with their friends, so that may change things too. So what you agree on at the beginning may no longer be appropriate or child focused, and I would recommend that the arrangements for your children should be reviewed annually.'

I asked Laura, 'What happens if you can't agree on child arrangements?'

'It's common for parents to disagree post-separation on what the appropriate arrangements should be for their children for various reasons,' she replied, 'but mainly because they have different interpretations of what is best for their children. Let's assume that you share parental responsibility for your children (the legal ability to be consulted about all your children's major life decisions, such as their education, their religious upbringing, their name, where they live and their healthcare). Then, if you both cannot reach an agreement about when your children should spend time with each of you – or any of the bigger life decisions, such as which school they should attend – you should try to use either solicitors to correspond for you or mediation. Mediation is where an independent third-party professional will assist you both in discussing the issues between you and communicating your respective opinions and in helping you to try to compromise and agree. If mediation is not suitable, or you still cannot reach agreement, then other options include arbitration, and, as a last resort, the court can be asked to make the decision for you. Court proceedings will take much more time and cost a lot of money (unless you qualify for legal aid), so this route should not be chosen before trying all non-court ways to first resolve your dispute.'

Separating as a co-habiting couple presents many challenges as well. While it rarely involves legal proceedings, there is still the matter of dividing up assets, money and children, both the human and furry kind.

I asked Laura about the legal differences between separating as a married couple and those who were unmarried, and she said, 'When you separate as co-habitees, obviously all the emotional side is the same, as is the advice about trying to be amicable and doing what's best for the children, but the legal process is different. If you're not married, there is nothing to dissolve, there's no legality to it and you can just walk away, without any formal process.'

'Financially it is very different, there are no laws that protect co-habitees, or any automatic rights. Just because you've been together six months or twenty years, there are no laws that give you rights, just by virtue of your relationship, unlike the matrimonial laws if you are married. This means you have no claims against each other's assets, unless they are specifically joint assets, or if you can show that you have an interest in the asset by providing evidence that you have made contributions to it.'

'If your house is solely owned by your partner, then you cannot claim any part of it, if you are not legally married or in a civil partnership. There is no law for co-habitees.

However, if you can evidence that you have made a significant financial contribution to the house, there you may have a chance of claiming some of it, but this is much harder than if you were married.'

'If you have a business together, then it would come down to what you have agreed or have in writing at the beginning of the business, so company law would apply to this, rather than matrimonial laws. Matrimonial laws will override what the company laws would say. If you are unmarried, but do have minor children together, you can claim financial provisions for the children, but nothing for yourself.'

Rosie Wilby told me, 'One tip for lesbians . . . during the relationship, stealthily "borrow" her clothes, especially things you look good in . . . then she'll probably say something like "oh, you can have that" . . . and you've sort of surreptitiously stolen all her stuff anyway by the time you break up!'

She added, 'Pet custody is a big topic for co-habiting gay couples . . . more of us have animals rather than human babies. Usually anyone who had the pet before the relationship started gets to keep it. If you got it together, the welfare of the pet should be taken into account. Which means: who has the best house and garden. And this is the reason I can't leave my current girlfriend. She has more money, so sadly would provide a better home for the "kids". Dammit.'

A wise friend once told me, you only get one chance to go through divorce and agree on the financial settlement, so you want to make sure you don't agree too quickly to anything, or feel bullied into stuff that doesn't feel right.

Part of the mediation and settlement process involved disclosing all of our bank statements, and any money we both had, to each other and the mediator. You should know there is a massive form, sexily called Form E, which is basically a long list of everything you have to your name. It was a FUCKING pain to complete, but very necessary and an integral part of the legal documentation for divorce. Sadly, reading through his bank statements revealed hurtful information, and that cut deep, even a year later. It was there in black and white, and brutal, but it was important to feel that rage and sense of injustice . . . to remember them . . . going into the negotiations.

Seeing my life in numbers and figures really hit home just how little I had saved, and how little I put in my pension. I felt vulnerable and stupid that I had gone from feeling secure and certain in a marriage and my future plans for retirement, to now being left not knowing how I was going to survive in my old age as a recently separated woman. I realised I needed to put on my big girl pants and learn more about money and to stop burying my head in the sand and being afraid of it, because, if I didn't learn about this stuff, who was going to do it for me now?

I am slightly embarrassed to say that until recently, I knew very little (SEE FUCK ALL) about budgeting, investments and pensions, even though I run two businesses and have worked my entire adult life. I know that lots of women are savvy when it comes to all of this, but I think I chose to ignore taking ownership of my own finances, because I was married and I naively thought I would be 'looked after' by him for the rest of my life. What a foolish mistake that was. Let me tell you now that talking about money, and getting to grips with how to ensure that you have made arrangements and plans for how you are going to survive in the future, is essential feminist work that all women must do. We shouldn't shy away from it, or rely on anyone else other than ourselves to understand, learn about and learn how to manage our own cash – especially those of us who become single later in life. It is never too late to learn.

Speaking openly about money has been a taboo, or seen as a 'vulgar' thing to do, for women, but this is slowly starting to change, especially through strong female voices on social media and online, such as Lynn Beattie aka Mrs Mummypenny. Lynn is the author of *The Money Guide to Transform Your Life* and writes about investing and budgeting for leading press. I sat down with her to have a frank chat and pick her brains about everything to do with cold hard cash and becoming single.

'It's still such a shameful subject to talk about,' Lynn said, 'and I really wish that it was different; and not just for women, for men as well. I just wish everybody could be more open about it. It's almost like the little parts of money – like saving money on your bills, or the best mortgage advisor to find – these kinds of things are talked about. However, when it comes to the bigger things – such as how much debt you are in and the feelings around debt, and sorting out money for the future, investing, where best to invest, how do you sort out your pension, and especially what happens to money when you die, which is another big taboo subject – none of these things are talked about.

'And often, in partnerships, money isn't talked about either, and so it can all bubble up into a nasty world of all these secrets, and differences with money as well; that can be something that causes a lot of issues as well, when two people have very different attitudes to money. One might be a huge splurger of money and one might be a huge saver and it leads to a lot of conflict, so I think we just need to be a lot more open about all forms of money. And have a chat with your friends and encourage them when you talk about it and then they'll talk about it. Have this honest conversation with other people and don't be scared of it.

'So yes, it's almost like you need to *start a relationship thinking about the end of a relationship* because we all know sadly that forty-two per cent of marriages end in divorce. People don't want to do it, they don't want to think about bad things happening, but it's protecting yourself and making sure that savings are equally split between two partners – pensions even can be split equally between partners – so it's having some foresight into what could happen in the future.'

I explained to Lynn that I was pretty much a teenager when it came to my knowledge of finances and budgeting; could she help me try to start to get my head around it, and what advice would she give to fellow single women? She calmly laid it out for me.

'One: Sit down one afternoon or evening, and get all your paperwork together and then plot it out on a spreadsheet, or just a piece of paper, as to where everything is at the moment. Start with the short-term stuff, the day-to-day bills, mortgage and household bills. Make sure you know all the money that's going out and all the different companies that it's going to.

'Two: Then start to look more at the medium-term things, like how much have you got in your emergency-fund money (hopefully you've got some emergency-fund money!). Three-to-six months' worth of salary is the figure we should all have sat there, for inevitable emergencies.

'Three: Get a handle on how much debt you've got, how much on credit cards, and loans and the interest rates and the repayments.

'Four: Then, have you got any money invested? Work out how much is there.

'Five: Have a look at your pension, get a valuation of it (and try not to freak out too much when you see it) because you're right, it can be a shock, but it's never too late to start putting money into it, and the earlier you can start the better.'

Doing this sounded very important, although I was incredibly frightened to see just how many times Deliveroo, or ASOS, or Figleaves lingerie was going to come up on my bank statement. In this first year of separation, I had done a lot of what Lynn called 'emotional spending', and it was time to actually open those bank statements and confront it, and perhaps even make a BUDGET. So what was Lynn's advice?

'When you're upset or angry, there's a tendency, especially for women, to spend as a kind of quick fix; it's almost like eating, or drinking – you spend to get that endorphin hit of that purchase, but then ten minutes later that's gone.

'A really great tool to use, to track how you're doing over a period of time, is a spending diary. I like to do it on a piece of paper and then I'll analyse it at the end of the week. I'll write down everything I spend, and that means literally everything; I mean every little odd cash transaction, whenever you use your current account, tapping to pay for things, when bills come out of your account and including PayPal. I also include things like business expenses as well – so, everything I was spending money on. Then I do some geeky work at the end of the week and put it all into a spreadsheet and put it into different categories, and then you can reflect back over the week, you know, like: On Tuesday I went to the supermarket and bought some alcohol, and then I made a big purchase on Amazon and I was feeling really awful that day. Then you can link up the spending to the emotion, and it just makes you aware of what you're doing. And I think once you recognise that you are spending in an emotional way, it's almost like it's one step towards getting in control of it.

'You might work out that you're spending three hundred pounds a month on groceries at the end of the month, so then there's no point in putting into your budget that that needs to be a hundred and fifty pounds, because that's too much of a cutback, but if you could maybe budget at two hundred pounds, or two hundred and fifty, then it makes it more realistic and easier to achieve. Then you have to have an allocation for fun money in your budget too. Don't forget to budget for fun, because, fuck, you've earned it.

'Once you've got your budget, that's when you can start to look at what costs can be reduced, and, I've said it before, but first of all get rid of the direct debits and the things that you really don't need – like, do you really need all of those subscriptions, such as Amazon Prime, Netflix, Disney Plus? You probably don't. Get rid of anything unnecessary. Get a better mobile phone deal, broadband deal, insurance deal. All these things take a bit of time, but, once you add them up you, could be saving yourself hundreds and hundreds of pounds, potentially thousands, if you've not done it for a while. And don't forget, if you're a single adult living in the house, you get a twenty-five per cent discount on your council tax, and you can backdate it. That can be worth hundreds of pounds in savings for you.'

Lynn ended our conversation by reassuring me that, even though it is a total faff getting my finances together, it is also empowering. She said, 'It's just nice being the only one that makes the decisions about what's around you, and not having to check the opinion of anybody else – it's all you.'

Lynn's parting words 'it's all you' echoed loudly with me and it was like I'd had an epiphany. Yes, YES, my life was going to be all about just me and my kids and this was exciting and powerful! I spent a lot of time during the divorce negotiations dreading that I was going to be on my own financially, but then I realised that every penny that I would earn from now on would just be for my new little family; no more sharing with him, no paying for someone else's gym membership, or holidays for four people, only three.

The main focus for me during the settlement and the mediation was to keep the kids in the house that had been their home. I had lived in this house for ten years, my son had been born in the lounge, and we had the most loving and caring neighbours who were like family. It was a cul-de-sac of cuddles and love, and there was no way I was going to move from it. I know I am in a very privileged position and that sadly for many people this is not the case, but I held tight to this and fought hard to make sure that the children didn't have to leave this special place.

Making sure I could afford to take on the house alone was down to whether or not the bank approved of a freelance comedian taking on the full responsibility. But it turns out that NatWest had a sense of humour and faith in me. On the day I called the bank and found out that I could take on the mortgage myself, I cried. I was forty-two years old, and after I paid out my ex's share, I could have a whole three-bedroom house to myself, and that was an enormous achievement. I remember calling Ellie and saying, 'Dude, you and I have worked really hard for eight years, and now I can own my own house and my children will be happy.' It was now time to start to move on, plan that divorce party and paint the kitchen pink.

Things I have learnt about money, separation and divorce

- Going into the separation, be as well informed as you can about your rights and the whole process; you only get one chance at this, and once everything is divided up and signed off, it is hard to change it.

- Hang in there. Don't feel you have to agree to things immediately; seek advice, or even just give yourself time to make decisions. It is an emotional and difficult time; give yourself a break if you need to.

- Money and talking about money is not scary, but having none when you retire is. Again, make sure you get to grips with how much you need to survive. The Gingerbread charity is a fantastic resource, and can inform you about benefits and child maintenance. And there are many online resources about getting yourself the right pension. YOU CAN DO THIS.

- Keep your cool, as much as you can. Find ways to keep your anger and frustrations contained during negotiations. Let out the anger after mediation meetings, or the difficult phone calls and emails, and don't let your ex rattle you.

- Try to be at peace with some compromises. It sucks not getting everything that you want, but to be free of a shitty relationship is pretty fucking sweet.

- Allow yourself to feel a bit sad at the end. It is such a big thing to go through, and you will have mixed emotions about it.

- Throw yourself a big fuck-off 'I'm Single' party. Celebrate this new fabulous life you have ahead of you.

8

Getting Stronger

When I talk about the impact of separation, I tend to bang on about the emotions, feelings and psychological aspects, but it was also my body that took a massive hit during the first year. In the initial stages, it ached, it held pain, produced tears and felt heavy. I pumped it full of booze, biscuits and bags of crisps, and, in the end, it got a bit (lot) angry with me. And as a consequence, there were days when I felt and looked 104 years old. Obviously, not everyone deals with break-ups like me. My other new single friends threw themselves into exercise and lost weight from the stress; I on the other hand put it on just by looking at a Jaffa Cake. But what was clear was that we all started to look and feel about our bodies in a new way; they were vessels full of possibility and freedom.

While it is obvious to say that my body has always belonged to me, and only me, being in a couple meant that I shared it intimately with another person (well, at least in the beginning). And now that he was out of the picture, it was just mine to enjoy and feel good about.

I know the terms 'loving yourself' and being 'body positive' get chucked around Instagram a lot, but it doesn't just happen from taking one hot yoga class or by buying a new lacy thong. And let's be honest, you don't have to love your body to appreciate it; just don't hate it, OK? It is like any other relationship: it develops and changes over time. There were days when I would be pissed off with it or hated how it moved and looked, or just how much fucking moustache hair grew out of it overnight. And that is more than all right. But one thing is for sure: there were moments when I was recovering from the separation, when I suddenly realised I was free to do anything I wanted with it. Absolutely anything! And that me and my body were free from comments, judgement or disapproval, and free to be whatever version of me I cared to be. I could pierce it, pluck it, sculpt it and learn to love it, even get a big tattoo of Dawn French on my arse if I wanted to. It was an exciting feeling to be so in control.

As I am writing this book, I am the biggest, hairiest and lumpiest and bumpiest I have ever been, but I have never felt more sexy or more alive! I love my body, and what it does for me, the way it feels, the way it wiggles when I dance alone in my kitchen to Lizzo, how it gets sweaty after a bike ride, and what it feels like when I hug a friend (when legally allowed to) who loves me. It's almost the exact opposite of how I thought I would feel after getting divorced. All the nonsense I believed about being in a couple and having a greater sense of worth was just lies, poisonous lies.

However, coming to this realisation has taken work, and a long time to unpick the layers of hate that I put on my body for many years. My relationship with my body has been fraught, to say the least. Growing up as a chubby child and then transforming into a very spotty teenager, who was also ravaged with stretch marks from head to toe, didn't make it easy to have a lot of blossoming self-confidence! My body looked nothing like anything that I saw on *Home and Away*. It was all wrong. The wrong shape and size and then packaged with terrible skin. There would be days when I wouldn't leave the house because my pimples were so bad, or that I felt I had nothing to wear to cover my body. I remember staring in the mirror and crying at my reflection, hating what I saw. How could anyone ever love me?

There were some moments and places I felt I could escape from those feelings, where I felt my body had some value and purpose, and that was on the stage and on the sports field. No surprises here, but I was a full dork and did all the school plays. On the stage, people just cared whether you could sing, or were funny, and it didn't matter if you were geeky, chubby or even spotty, because nothing covers pimples as well as that thick stage make-up.

And my netball team didn't care about looks, either. They needed me to block goals, not look pretty. Obviously, in netball I was a goal keeper (GK); it is the traditional fat girl position. And, even though I was a 'big girl', I was good at sport; not because I was thin or fast, or could jump backwards over a bar, but because I WAS STRONG! And yes, the only 'first' blue ribbon I ever got on sports day was for shot-put, because that is the law if you are my size and shape.

Even though my body felt amazing when I played sport, as soon as I got to university, I replaced sport with alcohol and cigarettes, and surprisingly I got a whole lot smaller from not eating as much. And, as a bonus, my skin cleared up and I discovered the power of my boobs. I didn't need to feel strong, and chuck a ball around a court, because suddenly boys paid me attention for two other reasons. So,

I gave up netball and replaced it with alcopops and tight tops.

I enjoyed trying to put as many different things in my body as possible, party drugs, weird cheap cocktails, and snogging and shagging a couple of men – and a few women, too. I remember one drunken night at college I even photocopied my tits. This was a time before smartphones. I put ten cents in the slot and flopped my jugs on the glass plate. DO NOT DO THIS. They looked like two fried ostrich eggs. And it was then I was mortified to discover I had actual hair growing out of my nipples.

In those early days of university, I loved my body because of the way people looked at me and what it felt like to be fancied, but this was a very short-lived time. While it should have been the start of my experimental twenties, I changed all that by meeting the 'love of my life' at the beginning of my second year at uni, and that was it . . . me and my body, loved, happy, sorted, done, right?

Fast forward twenty years, and after giving birth to two massive babies and again being covered in even more stretch marks and a growing number of skin tags and random hair, I decided I better do something about this human flesh lump I was carrying around. Like a lot of people when they hit middle age, I started to freak out and set some wildly unrealistic fitness goals. The year I turned the big Four Zero, I took up running, because that is what people like me do. Was I completely slow, ungraceful, and barely moving, yes! Did that matter? Not one bit. Did I love that I could move my size 18 body? Yup, you betcha.

However, I am not a natural runner, and had to really work on that inner voice that I had harboured since I was a teenager, that I was both slow and not made for this sport.

Our experience of health and fitness at high school has a huge impact on our relationship with it as adults. In 2019, I recorded a podcast series called *Fat Lot of Good*, and I interviewed over twenty guests about how they felt about their bodies over the course of their lives. Time and time again, both women and men would discuss how negatively they felt about exercising because of how they were pigeonholed or put off by a PE teacher and made to feel they weren't good enough. So many believed that their body type couldn't run, or they were too big or, conversely, too fragile for certain activities. Shaking off those words and feelings is as big a step forward as is actually getting outside and doing something positive for your body. But slowly, slowly I began to change this narrative for myself.

And dear God, and I became THAT friend, that running bore. Off I would plod on the weekends, around my local parks, posting about it on social media – because, if it's not on Instagram, it didn't happen. I was literally just putting one foot in front of the other and doing a bouncy walk, but I was running, and suddenly I was doing something I never thought a chunky mother of two could achieve. I did exercise for how it made me feel, rather than how it made me look, and I started to appreciate my body for what it was capable of doing. I got the 'runner's high' or 'runner's smugness', as Ellie likes to call it.

Then one day I got a call out of the blue from the writer and all-round brilliant human Bryony Gordon, who asked me and Ellie if we wanted to run the London Marathon. See, all that boasting on social media DID pay off. We would get a media place, and could run with a bunch of amazing women IN OUR PANTS. What's not to love about that? We had a quick think about it and then went fuck it, why not? We like a challenge and we definitely love attention. Bryony assured us that if she could run it, so could we. So that was that: the Scummy Mummies were going to run a bloody long way.

Run 26.2 miles; that sounds like a laugh, doesn't it? Definitely the same as a sluggish 5km Park Run. Turns out you can do it; it just means you are just running, and talking about running, all the time. When you're not doing that, you're buying stupid whizzy sport watches, applying chafing cream, and carb loading. I would definitely do it again, just for the spaghetti carbonara. Training was hours and hours of plodding around the streets of London, in all weathers and getting the miles done. But I was doing it; all fifteen stone of me was GOING TO RUN A MARATHON.

I was fully committed to this new aspect of my life. I joined several Facebook groups and witnessed the most uplifting messages of encouragement and support. This huge online community of female runners was absolutely inspiring. One of the women I met through my running circle was Emma Campbell, aka @limitless_em, an author and campaigner who has had three cancer diagnoses, as well as going through separation six months after giving birth to triplets. I asked Emma what running meant to her. She said, 'Running helps me minimise the emotional impact cancer would otherwise have on my life. It shows me, every single day, that I am strong, resilient and capable of overcoming the darkest of times.' And it was stories like Emma's and hundreds of other women that kept me motivated and feeling part of an important movement of incredible humans.

During those big training months, I ADORED my body; it felt amazing, powerful and capable of doing this BIG THING. I was now a fat 41-year-old, and I felt I was finally getting free of the negativity I had carried for so many years. While I had gained confidence through stand-up, there was something about achieving a seemingly impossible physical goal that made me respect my body.

We were scheduled to run the London Marathon on 4 April 2020, and we had detailed training plans all working towards this. The big practice for me was the Vitality Big Half on the 1st of March, and I couldn't wait to do this. As I mentioned in the chapter The Decision, my ex also ran in the race, but, on the day, I ran the whole way with the West End musical star, Carrie Hope Fletcher. Side by side, we jogged our way around the streets of the capital. As we made our way around the course to enormous cheers, people shouted, 'Go Carrie!', to her and, 'Keep Going!', to me. Next time, I'm writing my name on my back! When we crossed the finishing line, I cried and felt so damn proud. In just under three hours, I had made my body move thirteen miles and was on the verge of running an actual marathon. I felt high; I felt like I was invincible. However, all this changed four days later, when I found what had happened.

I stopped running. I stopped moving. I crashed.

In the first few weeks of the separation, all I wanted to do was numb the feelings inside. I was soothed by Sauv Blanc; I was comforted by Cabernet . . . I just wanted to stop hurting. I had always been a social smoker, but I decided to up this to a more professional level during the bleak days. Marlboro Greens, thanks, for minty freshness. I had my trusty smoking jacket that I kept by the door, which smelled amazing. I would wear it so the kids couldn't smell the smoke on me when I had snuck outside for a secret puff. I would then rush inside and wash my hands and face and brush my teeth. They didn't notice. I was a smoking ninja.

The other thing my body felt was rejected and disgusting. When somebody hurts you in a way that shows they didn't love you, it triggers all the negative memories of the past.

You go back over the times that they touched you and think, 'Did they actually mean that hug? Did they really want me? Did he ever think I was beautiful? Am I beautiful? Will anyone ever desire me? I AM THE ONE HE DIDN'T WANT.' Yuck, yuck, fucking yuck.

My own opinion about my body may have suddenly taken a nosedive, but how others saw me did not. All my girlfriends said brilliantly uplifting things like: 'You are sexy!'; 'You are loved!'; 'It's his loss, babes!'. All gorgeous, but I needed to start believing it. I realise that all these negative feelings were all part of the process of grief, and that following the shock, sadness and denial, it was time to get angry. And stronger.

The first steps towards getting better were about being gentle to myself. I started to do one-to-one classes with my Pilates teacher, Suzy. Saturday mornings, I would call her up on Zoom and just breathe and stretch. I spent so much of my time huddled over my phone or contorted on the sofa, I needed an hour to stretch out. It was surprisingly good to start the weekends just lying on a mat thinking about my pelvic floor! Although on more than one occasion, there were times where I had to stop the class to go and vomit because I was so hungover. Classy, Thorn, really classy.

It was weird going from being this beacon of good marathon running health to a borderline alcoholic who was doing her best to earn herself a lung transplant. I knew it wasn't sustainable, but I just kept going. I had built both a professional and personal reputation as being that fun 'boozy mate'. I took photos of myself holding glasses of wine and put them on social media, and the women who followed me cheered me along. 'Wine time' became pretty much all the time!

During the school summer holidays, about five months after the split, we decided we would both take the kids away for two weeks each. I had them first, and then it was time to hand them over to their dad. There were mixed feelings – I felt so incredibly protective of them, and us as a family of three – but they were soon replaced with the joy of knowing I could live like a 21-year-old for the entire time. I booked in a 'drunch' (drunken lunch) for most days, and dinners out with friends. I lined up a few dates with a couple of men from Tinder and felt elated that I was free from responsibilities. I wanted to prove to everyone that I was fun, single and that good-time girl everyone wanted to get pissed with.

I stayed up late either drinking with friends or – on the nights I wasn't doing that – having sex with men. I managed to have four one-night stands in two weeks. As I explain in the Sex chapter, it was easy: swipe right; chat; organise to meet in a pub and if they weren't a murderer or a Tory, then ding dong, go home for sex. It made me feel like my body was alive and desired. Surely, this was what I needed; this was part of getting better. It felt good to be reckless and promiscuous. It was safe consensual sex with another grown-up.

But after a week of no sleep and putting all manner of things in and out of my body, I began to spin a bit out of control. On day eight of my bender, I met a friend at a fancy club in East London. We sat down for lunch at 1pm and quickly threw back three bottles of wine, and then some cocktails. I hadn't seen her since the separation and relayed everything in gory detail. We got more pissed, cried, she got out her Tarot cards and told me that my life was about to get great. The world kept spinning, faster. And then we decided to go for a swim in the rooftop pool. It was getting close to five o'clock, but by this stage I could hardly stand or see.

After the swim (and possibly a snog), I put on my jumpsuit without a bra – which is always a great look when you have G-cup breasts! – and we both managed to stumble out of the club. I remember it was 5.30pm. I just needed to get home, I thought. I was determined to take the train, I've no idea why. And I sort of remember being at the station, and then the next thing I knew, I was standing on a street with vomit on my shoes and then I smashed into a pole and split my lip open. I vaguely remember a woman saying, 'Is that Helen from the Scummy Mummies?', and me waving her away. And then the rest is BLANK.

My poor friends who were meant to be meeting me at my house for dinner (I was supposed to be cooking for them) were now outside my front door and I was nowhere to be found. They asked my neighbours, but they had no idea. They called Ellie, and then everyone panicked. I was lost and my phone had run out of battery. They walked around the local area, called the friend I had been with and she told them I had headed home. No one had a clue where I was.

At 9pm, my neighbours, who had a key, decided to check inside my house, where they found me passed out on my sofa. I have absolutely no idea how I got home or what happened for three hours, but I was safe and very, very drunk, and then very ashamed. All of this because I couldn't say no to just one more glass of wine. I felt embarrassed and I hated myself for what I had done to those who had carried me through my darkest hours. I was broken, and a little bit scared of what could have happened in those missing hours. Where the hell had I been? Did anyone touch me? As the comedian Amy Schumer famously said, 'Nothing good ever happens in a blackout. I've never woken up and been like, "What is this Pilates mat doing out?"'

Two days later, after sobering up, did I just drink green tea and have a kale salad? Nope. Ridiculously, I booked myself in for a full fanny wax, which I had never done before in my life. I thought by making myself bald as a badger in my nether regions I would somehow feel sexier. I mean, having the hair ripped out of your private parts by a stranger is always a confidence boost, right? So, now that I felt silky smooth down there, I thought it was a great idea to go on another date! As luck would have it, I actually ended up meeting up with a lovely man, who I later affectionately called the West London Tripod, for obvious reasons, and we ended up going back to his place. We stayed up until 5am drinking, getting stoned and shagging all night. I got that hit of attention and that buzz of irresponsibility and recklessness. It was intoxicating in all senses of the word. I slept forty-five minutes in total. As the alcohol wore off, the sun rose. I got dressed and stumbled out of his place at 9am. I remembered I had to catch a train to Northampton in the afternoon and I still needed to get home.

I took the tube home, make-up all over my face, wearing a sequinned jacket. I got to Canada Water station, and, while I was on the escalator, I heard, 'Helen! Helen!'

I looked up, and my friend Victoria and her ten-year-old son were metres away, coming towards me.

She instantly realised I was on my way home, rather than going out for the day. 'Where have you been?' she asked with a smirk.

'Umm . . . just getting home,' I said, like I was a 19-year-old university student, brimming with confidence. My friend gave me a knowing look and nod, and I felt a mix of pride and disgust.

By the afternoon, I was on my way to Northampton to see some girlfriends. I bought two bottles of wine and several tins of gin and lots of junk food, fuel to keep me awake and buzzing. We were going to be having another boozy night and session in the hot tub afterwards. Perfect; nothing could possibly go wrong.

I arrived and started to chain-smoke and drink. Even though I hadn't slept, I felt pretty buoyed from seeing loved ones. We drank and ate and then popped into the hot tub. Warm, bubbly water, after all that alcohol, meant I instantly wanted to fall asleep. I kept splashing my face and rubbing my eyes to stay awake. And then suddenly, my friend turned to me and said, 'Holy fuck, what's happened to your eye?'

The next morning I woke and tried to open my eyes, except only the right one would. I gave the left one a rub, and felt the bulging lid; it was like freshly waxed fanny or a marshmallow made of flesh. Oh fuck! My body had finally cracked the shits with me and was shouting at me to say, 'FFS Helen, just STOP!' I walked downstairs, and my friend began to laugh, saying, 'See, something was wrong with your eye!' There was no hiding that my body was giving up on me.

It was my brother's birthday in Australia that morning and I had to Zoom my whole family from my friend's house. When they saw me, they collectively went, 'Eeeewwwww.' My siblings are amazing.

I explained I had just been in a hot tub, but neglected to mention the excessive drinking and shagging I had been getting up to.

My left eye stayed like that for TWO MONTHS, but this didn't stop me from still trying to have a sex life. I had a couple of dates where I just styled my hair over my face, but, surprisingly, that didn't seem to work. And on one particularly special daytime date, I turned up in a pair of Jackie O-inspired sunglasses, a sophisticated disguise, but my potential bed buddy at the end of our meet-up said, 'I'll come back and fuck you when your eye isn't gammy!' Thanks, Casanova. In a last-ditch attempt for late-night nooky, I bought a lacy Gabrielle-inspired eyepatch, and asked a potential lover if he was into pirate role play. 'Aye, aye, captain,' he said.

Nothing would fix it. I went to pharmacies, saw doctors online, bought drops, wipes and washed it with baby shampoo, and someone on Instagram even offered to give me some of her breast milk to apply to it. My 'fanny eye' even became a running joke with the Scummy Mummies followers. Then, finally, I took myself to Moorfields Eye Hospital. (Why didn't I just go there first?) On my second visit there, I spent six hours having blood tests, scans and seeing several doctors. There was an infection and a lump going on behind my eye, I was told, and they had to operate within a couple of days to find out what it was. One of the things they were testing me for was syphilis . . . SYPHILIS! I broke down and sobbed out of my good eye in a Costa. I was feeling the most alone I had in months. I had let my body down and I was broken. I suddenly didn't want to be single any more. I wanted to be scooped up by someone who loved me and held me, but, the truth is, I wasn't alone at all. A few days later, I came back to the hospital for my eye surgery. One of the biggest achievements of the day was that I fasted until 6pm, an extraordinary bodily feat for me. I tried not to think about the surgeon cutting open my eyelid, or what was going to happen to me under anaesthetic, and instead concentrated on thoughts of the sweet, sweet opiates I was going to get.

When I awoke from the surgery, I got a huge surprise: Ellie was sitting by my bed, along with my big brother John. She had come to take me home. She had been doing some work close by and then spontaneously decided to visit me. She was all dolled up in fabulous clothes, and when the nurse came in, she said to me, 'Isn't it lovely your daughter came to visit you!' YOUR DAUGHTER. I nearly popped my eye stitches from laughing. Ellie will never let me forget that comment.

In a few weeks, my eye was finally back to normal, and I am happy to announce I was syphilis free. BONUS.

I asked the psychologist Dr Rachel Master about whether I needed this crash to happen.

She said, 'Sometimes we need to get to "rock bottom" before we are forced to confront the hard stuff. I think so many of us go through life pushing away painful feelings. But this strategy is never sustainable! Ultimately you burn yourself out. Our bodies often are what forces us to stop. Migraine. Autoimmune reactions (your eye!) or crippling fatigue. I think the crash you speak of is ultimately a gift, as you finally have no choice but to accept and sit with the truth. Process the grief, the losses, the sadness. And then you emerge a more full-bodied and richer version of yourself.'

The two books that I read at the time that had a big influence on me and helped me sort my shit out were by the author Catherine Gray. *The Unexpected Joy of Being Single* and *The Unexpected Joy of Being Sober* are so raw and honest, and never shied away from the darkness of alcohol and dating. Catherine's story of recovering from alcohol addiction and the crashes she had before she got sober hit home. As Catherine says, 'I didn't have a drinking problem as such. I was great at drinking! It was the stopping. I had a stopping problem.' I could see I was on my way to having my own serious problem, so reading her book was exactly what I needed to stop me spiralling down any further. Her stories of online dating and the endless scrolling through the apps and craving those dopamine hits from matching and texting rang scarily true with me, too. Catherine's powerful stories made me question what was I getting from booze and sex and how I was abusing my body. I needed to dry out, in more ways than one, and I needed a team of brave women to help me.

So it was time to face my relationship with my body, and alcohol and sex, and stop flashing my foof around so much, and to get better, stronger and sober.

In the summer, I got an email from a local personal trainer, Suzanne, who wondered if I wanted to come in for some weight training with her at her all-female gym. She was a big fan of the podcast and wanted to know if she could get me fit. 'Yes!' I said. This was exactly what I needed; there was no way I was going to fix myself alone. I needed someone to put me back together and rebuild me.

I had been curious about weight training ever since I'd watched the comedian Jessica Fostekew perform her incredible show *Hench* at the Edinburgh Fringe in the summer of 2019. Jess's show recounts her experiences about getting strong through weight training, and the way women's bodies are judged, especially by arsey men at the gym. The poster for the show was a powerful image of Jess looking straight at the camera in lifting gear and holding a massive barbell. I asked Jess about how weight lifting helped when she was going through her separation. She said, 'I think, more than ever, during times like break-ups, when your heart is broken, it's a different kind of exercise then; it's a different type of adrenaline. I think you're kind of clawing for some connection with yourself. It is the most connected to myself that I've ever felt; it felt like freedom. I think that's the best way to describe it.' And this is what I needed in my next steps to recovery; I felt so disconnected from my body, and I needed to claim it back.

On the first morning I met Suzanne, I arrived twenty minutes late because I was so hungover. Good start. Suzanne sat me down and made me a strong coffee. This was exactly the type of gym workout I was after. We talked about what my goals were: basically, 'lift heavy shit' and 'not be dead'. I was honest about how physically and emotionally broken I was, and that any help to get me out of this shithole would be wonderful. She wrote down some notes (that probably said 'absolute disaster') and told me she could help.

We agreed that I should probably start seeing her weekly. She would make me bench press and deadlift heavy weights, and concentrate on my non-existent pelvic floor muscles, which she affectionately called the 'jellyfish'. While I was doing my squats and lunges, I would tell her about my terrible dating exploits in detail and just how much I had been drinking on the nights without the kids. It was like therapy and exercise combined. Sorry, Suzanne, you really didn't need to hear about all of THAT. As the weeks went by, I could see a change in how I was carrying myself; I walked up stairs without aching, I got out of bed more easily, and I would get giddy about how much I would lift in the next session. It was becoming addictive. I was getting so high off how much I could lift, it felt like I had experienced a religious conversion and I was becoming a true believer.

Suzanne had worked with women from teenagers to those in their eighties, who had come to this type of exercise for many reasons. I asked her why she thought weight training was so important and healing.

'One of the biggest aspects of going through shock and trauma,' she told me, 'is the damage to the nervous system. And in turn we see this expose itself in the body and mind. It's like the body and mind need the time, space and right elements of recovery to come back. Weight training is one of those elements and we find it is instrumental in healing and recovery. It all starts with learning how to breathe and how to link the breath to the pelvic floor, then using this to build strength and power from the inside out. Weight training can feel spiritual because it gives you back the time and energy to focus on just you.'

I was interested to know how she approached me when I arrived in such a terrible mess.

'When you first started weight training,' she said, 'we focused on slowing down, getting your nervous system to move calmly and gradually introducing heavier weights. This is hard because you are strong and powerful! You displayed incredible physical and emotional strength and were willing to push hard in every workout or session. So, as a trainer, to risk doing the opposite is to risk upsetting and demotivating somebody. Luckily for me, you knew this stuff and understood that weight training, like all training, should be restorative, gradually building and progressing in all aspects. Giving one hundred per cent doesn't and shouldn't mean trashing your body in every training session. It means handing yourself over and trusting the process. Seeing these notable positive mental and physical changes in you has been awesome, but they have not always come easy. I am sure you won't mind me saying that there have been many emotional training sessions. Swearing, shouting and crying and laughing . . . but weight training tends to have that effect.'

It was this explosive impact of the training that felt the most satisfying. There was one particular morning when everything in me just erupted. I told Suzanne about why my marriage had broken down, and I could feel the rage starting to bubble, but instead of letting these feelings overwhelm and weaken me, I used the anger to power my muscles. It was primal and raw. With each sentence and painful memory I brought up, I would pump the heavy weights. 'And then he did this!' POW. 'And he said this!' WHAM. 'He was such a fucking bastard!' BOOM. Harnessing the rage within myself and converting it to strength was beyond healing; it was powerful. Those endorphins flooded my body. MY BODY WAS COMING BACK! And coming back fiercer and braver than it had ever been.

Poorna Bell, journalist and the author of the amazing book *Stronger*, writes about the impact that becoming a competitive powerlifter had on both her body and self-confidence, and her recovery from grief. She talked to me about the changes she saw in herself, and that it was 'two things; one was about seeing how much weight I could lift, but also what that did for my confidence, and I'm not just talking about confidence when you go into the gym, I'm talking about confidence when I walked down the street, or going into a meeting, or when I'm running an event, or whatever those things might be, and I thought that that was incredible.

'And then when I made that realisation, because literally the next day after I did my first competition I noticed that difference in how I held myself and walked and so on. It's a very neutral strength: you're not walking down the street trying to pick a fight; you're walking down the street and you own that space. And what I noticed was, because of how we've been conditioned – men and women are conditioned, and women are conditioned to shrink themselves, to take up as little space as possible – was that act of being able to have ownership of space that I'm around. There is a silent communication that happens between your body language and other people, so you don't have to always constantly re-enforce, or fight for it.

'So what I noticed was that first day I walked down the street, I saw this group of guys coming towards me, and usually what I would have done was lower my eyes; I would have looked at the pavement and walked against the wall or moved out of their way. But this time I didn't move out of the way; I just kept walking. And what then happened . . . they just moved around me. They just parted and moved around me. And there wasn't tension and there wasn't aggression; it was just about holding your space.'

Finding the right type of exercise for you after a break-up is important, and I would say essential for healing. As Helen Russell told me, 'We all know the positive mental and physical benefits of exercising, but actually what I found really interesting researching my book *How to Be Sad* was that actually *not exercising* can make you feel sad very quickly, and randomised control trials show that if you don't move, after a week you will feel worse. So, that almost flipped it on its head for me, because I was like, "Yeah, I know I should exercise," but then thinking, "Oh, if I don't do this, it's going to feel a lot worse."'

In *How to be Sad*, Helen writes, 'Even when we're not suffering from depression, exercise can stop normal sadness and low moods tipping into something more serious. In 2018, Brendon Stubbs and his colleagues did a meta-analysis and found that exercise decreases the risk of developing depression, regardless of age and geographical region. "We found that higher levels of physical activity were protective against future depression in children, adults and older adults," says Stubbs, "across every continent and after taking into account other important factors, such as body mass index, smoking and physical health conditions." In 2020, Stubbs and his colleagues published new research confirming that light activity is also good for preventing mental health problems in teenagers. The evidence now exists, in black and white, that exercise works to both prevent depression and help treat it.'

So, if you are thinking about what types of exercise are right for you, here are my top tips for exercising after separation.

Post Break-up Exercise Tips

- **Walking –** OK, so this is bloody obvious, but going for long walks when you're feeling sad does make you feel better, so much better. Going out with someone is great for your mental health, too. If you can't get a friend to join you, I found downloading a soothing audio book, or just playing your favourite tunes, lifts a mood even more. I got to the point where I stopped caring that I was singing Kylie's 'Spinning Around' loudly as I meandered around my local park, and that felt amazing.

- **Swimming –** Just being in water is like being hugged. While I haven't got into the whole cold water thing, getting in the sea, or taking a dip in your local pool, is so nourishing, and also the next best thing to having a massage (and a fraction of the cost). Even just doing a few gentle laps up and down the lanes stretches out your body and gives you all those lovely endorphins. And remember, nobody cares what you look like in your swimsuit, and no, you don't have to shave either.

- **Yoga and Pilates –** You don't have to be a stick-thin twenty-something in a crop top to enjoy both of these wondrous activities. I love that most of the classes involve either just breathing or lying down, I mean, this is the kind of exercise I like and am good at. And taking time to get your pelvic floor in better shape is always a good thing too. There are plenty of free ones to do online, and all have beginners classes for even the most inflexible and curvy bodies. My favourites are 'Yoga with Adriene' and 'Jessamyn Stanley'. Dump all those preconceived ideas about touching your toes or standing on your head. Doing yoga and Pilates is just as much about taking time out for yourself as it is downward dogging.

- **Boxing –** It goes with saying that having the chance to punch and bash at something (safely) and get out your anger and rage is HUGELY beneficial. I did a few classes and felt instantly better. Yes, those gloves get sweaty and smelly, but get among it, release all those negative feelings and turn them into brilliant, powerful energy. And, yup, it is compulsory that you play 'Eye of the Tiger' while you do it.

- **Weight Training –** As I mentioned, this type of exercise was the most transformative for me and my body. Through weight training, I made myself physically and mentally stronger, and this was so important for my recovery. Lifting heavier and heavier weights each week was so motivating, and I felt so proud when I could deadlift a massive barbell. Again, there are classes online and you can even use homemade weights like soda bottles in your house.

- **HIIT –** These are short, super energetic, and super sweaty workouts that get your heart racing and your body pumping. You can do a 15- or even a 7-minute workout and feel incredible for the rest of the day, or just smug. When you are time poor, these are a brilliant way to get some oxygen around your body, and you don't have to leave your house to do them. Joe Wicks has wonderful short classes on YouTube, and even just watching his happy little face can perk you up.

- **Dancing –** This has got to be my favourite kind of exercise and one that doesn't feel like a 'workout'. Just picking a few banging tunes to get that bottom wiggling is so energising and fun. Often it would be the first thing I did after the kids went away for the weekend, as a circuit breaker for feeling sad or lonely. Bananarama's 'Venus' or Sylvester's 'You Make Me Feel (Mighty Real)' are my go-to feel-good tracks.

These are just a few examples, but find something that suits you and your budget. You don't need to spend a lot of time or money; any bit of movement can make a huge difference when you are recovering and getting your mojo back.

Now that my body was re-forming, it was time to sort out my relationship with booze. I knew that I had to have a break from wine; that was bloody obvious. So I rang an Aussie mate called Nikki, who is a nutritionist, and asked for help. She patiently listened as I told her how debauched I had been and how I was falling into a booze-soaked heap. To break out of the cycle, she suggested I go on a 21-day cleanse, and said that she would text me every day and support me through it. Sure. I was to give up wheat, dairy, caffeine and alcohol, for THREE FUCKING WEEKS. I hadn't gone without wine since I was pregnant. My body was pretty much a cheese and carbohydrate sculpture in human form. But, I thought, if I got through the first months of separation during a global pandemic, I could get through anything.

I know the words 'cleanse' or 'detox' conjure images of Gwyneth Paltrow looking smug while lighting her own vagina-scented candle, but I felt I needed to stop relying on Pinot Grigio when my emotions felt out of control. It was too easy to pour myself a glass when I got a text message from my ex. It was also completely off-brand to the party girl image I was so often portraying on social media, but I had to stop thinking of what others would think of me.

I started the cleanse, like I did with all the other millions of diets I have tried in the last twenty years, with stupidly blind optimism: 'This is the new me'; 'I love kale'; 'I will just make good choices for me' . . . and then, after about three days, I start getting bored, and just want to either cry or scoff handfuls of Babybels straight from the fridge.

The biggest hurdle was coffee. FUCK ME, the first few days felt like I was actually going to murder someone. The headaches, the tiredness and the jittery anxiety were shocking. I found myself sniffing coffee beans to get a hit. I usually drink about five cups of coffee a day, so to go to zero was evil. But I persisted and tried delicious things like decaf (the devil's water) and green tea (piss). The absence of wheat and dairy seemed relatively easy as I was too busy having sexual thoughts of fellating a cappuccino.

I decided I would announce my cleanse online, because I am a bit needy, but also because I thought if I told 140k strangers I was doing it, there might be a bit of accountability (attention), and I would actually get it done. After I blurted it all out, I was heartened by how many women had attempted similar detoxes, and how most people agreed that quitting coffee was like giving up oxygen. This gave me the strength to continue. The last three days of cleanse were going to be at a yoga retreat with my friend Emily. I thought, fuck it, why not end my wanky cleanse in full wankery. Just to be clear, I am the LEAST bendy, least yoga-y person I know; I can barely sit cross-legged, but one of the superpowers of being single and separated means you are open to new adventures (see humiliation).

Before becoming separated, I wouldn't have been brave enough to put myself in a room full of gorgeous (thin) women, who made downward dogging look like ballet. It felt exposing. So much of what I do is about taking the piss out of myself, and this was a little bit serious, and calm and quiet. It was scarier than standing on stage in a gold catsuit. This was about being vulnerable, and also being comfortable about farting in front of a room full of strangers.

When the first class started, I did that thing I shouldn't: I noted that I was definitely the fattest, was the worst at yoga, and there was no bloody way I was standing on my head. 'Oh

God, everyone will be looking at me, judging me.' But once we were off . . . nobody cared. Nobody looked sideways. And even though I looked more like a drunken hen dancing to 'YMCA' most of the time, I managed to do a few warrior poses and cobras. Get me and the lingo.

By the end of the weekend, I felt elated. I had finished my 21-day cleanse. I had got through hard things without a drop of wine, and I had stayed awake without the prop of a single flat white. I was standing, just as I am, a rebuilt Helen. I felt in control.

Before we headed back to London, my friend Emily suggested that we find the closest beach and swim in the sea. Holkham beach was about a 40-minute drive away, and I had visited there years before with my ex-husband and young daughter. I remembered the endless sky and the open beach and craved that full force of nature on my senses. When you feel broken, there is almost comfort in feeling like you are part of something enormous – that there is more out there than your sadness among the expanse of beauty.

It was still sunny and almost warm, for English standards, so about 17 degrees. Holkham beach in Norfolk is famous for having the longest sand dunes and being a place of 'outstanding beauty'. We made the 20-minute trek from the endless car park to the soft sandy beaches – we were determined to 'get in the sea'. As luck would have it, it was windy and grey skyed, but we stripped off anyway and headed into the bracing cold water. And, oh my, the waves bashed at me and my body – it was thrilling, icy and exciting. Maybe this is what all those cold water swimmers keep talking about? It was satisfying, like really good sex after a drought. It felt triumphant after I had got through weeks without alcoholic props, cheese binges and carbs. I had nourished, rather than punished myself. I had loved all of me. And I had realised I was capable of healing myself, and that I deserved it.

I would love to say that I was fully converted to a sober life, or that I never ate a Big Mac, or sucked down a Marlboro again, or that I never had a one-night stand and flashed my bush at a man I met on the internet, but, frankly, that is not me. What I learnt from going through a period of abusing my body, and letting it be broken, is that it is tougher than I thought and that I could survive, but also, that I was worthy of love, and that love came in many forms. I knew that I was going to be happier and more fulfilled, and that I would never go a day without coffee ever again.

Things I have learnt about my body and exercise

- You do not have to be a certain size or look a particular way to exercise or enjoy your body. As soon as I let go of what I thought my size 18 body could and couldn't do, I opened myself up to the most fulfilling experiences, as well as a community of badass women.

- Move your body every day. It is so ridiculously simple, and I hope I am not telling you the fucking obvious here, but even having a dance in your kitchen while making dinner is a pretty nice way of loving yourself. And enjoy those sweet, sweet endorphins.

- Drinking lots of booze is a temporary way to numb yourself from the pain of separation, but it is not sustainable and can be incredibly dangerous, as I discovered. Developing a healthy relationship with alcohol is vital for both your physical and mental health.

- Takeaways and junk food are fucking amazing, but only up to a point. Allow yourself to eat the crap at the beginning without guilt, but, when you're ready, it is good to have a few vegetables here and there to balance out the pizza. Surprisingly, healthy food DOES make you feel better; who knew?

- Take your body out on a date with itself. I know this sounds cheesy, but have a night or afternoon when you give yourself everything you love. For me it's a bath, carbonara, *Schitt's Creek* and a wank, but you do you.

- Oh, and NEVER GET IN A HOT TUB.

9

Getting my Sexual Mojo Back and the Joys of Wanking

OK, here we go; we are all grown-ups here.

One of the absolute joys of becoming single has been rediscovering sex – and I mean the good stuff; the wonderful, glorious, toe-curling, orgasmatron-inducing all-night banging. Oh dear lord, why didn't anyone tell me about how good it could actually be? Seriously, after spending twenty-one years with the same man, and having an 'OK' sex life, I had no idea that I could feel this amazing or that I could feel this desirable, or even, in fact, that great feminist term, 'fuckable'. It has been truly transformational.

While I have eaten up this new aspect of my life like I was at a delicious all-you-can-eat cock buffet, beyond the physical pleasures, getting back into sex was a huge step towards me recognising my complicated relationship with men and what my behaviours were like around them. The transition from 'wife' to 'lover' has been an eventful one, to say the least. The interactions I have begun to have with men have been an opportunity to be free to explore pleasure and flirting, and to become adventurous and assertive in my own right. Sex was no longer loaded with the expectations of 'maintaining' a long-term relationship, or just going through a routine, firmly entrenched in the well-trodden familiar. I have had to learn to unpick and undo my hang-ups about my sexual self and reframe, rebuild and enjoy a much more fulfilling sex life that was just for me this time round.

My entry back into the world of sex has predictably been one of mishaps, mistakes and misadventure. When I was ready, I jumped into the heady wilds of online dating and got myself a few excellent shags, quick smart. So many of my initial apprehensions I had about my body and sexuality quickly disappeared, as I realised that it was only me who was being judgemental of my body and not my lovers. What was even more exciting than drunken one-night stands was the fact that the breakdown of my marriage allowed me to reawaken my desire and a libido that had been hidden for years in the back of the kitchen cupboard (somewhere near the Tupperware lids): suddenly I felt *sexual*.

While getting properly laid is magnificent, to be honest, the best bit was just feeling 'turned on' again. Having some top-quality sex with myself made me feel renewed and pretty bloody jolly. I'm not saying I wanked myself happy (well, I might be), but working out how to give *myself* amazing orgasms certainly has added a spring to my single step and a glow to my divorced face. I just wish I had worked this out a lot sooner! What a waste of twenty-odd years!

When it comes to masturbation, I am definitely a late bloomer, but JESUS, I have made up for lost time. Now that I have a couple of days a week alone, I have this wonderful NEW opportunity to explore this part of my sexuality. Oh, the joy of an orgasm first thing in the morning, or in the shower, or just because I feel like it on a sunny afternoon (or even a rainy one). I have bought adventurous sex toys and umpteen lubes and got to know exactly how I can give myself an almighty good time in just three minutes and I now know that five wanks in a night is my maximum (what a sweaty night of self-love that was).

Tragically, when I was a teenager, I thought wanking was just for boys and only really experienced a fairly mediocre orgasm when I was with someone else. In my twenties and thirties, I think I only made myself climax a handful of times (pun intended). It wasn't until I hit forty that I really began to explore self-pleasure. Being a comedian and on tour a lot meant that I had more time to get jiggy alone. This was partly spurred on by being given vibrators as a gift, one from a group of girlfriends for my 40th birthday, and the other, funnily enough, from a leading psychologist and self-help coach, called Dr Pam Spurr (pun not my fault).

Pam gave both Ellie and me these vibrating 'bullets' when she was our expert guest on the 'Sex Episode' on *The Scummy Mummies Podcast*. At the time, I remember being hugely embarrassed, and slightly uncomfortable, but tried to hide it. But that little vibrator was to be a complete game changer for me. I took it to every hotel. It was (practically) the size of a lipstick and I could pack it in my make-up bag. Who knew such a small thing would have such a big impact on my burgeoning wanking career?

I decided to get in touch with Dr Spurr, as she has written extensively about sex and pleasure in books and the media, because I wanted to ask her why masturbation was so important for self-confidence and getting back into sex after a separation. She explained that, 'self-pleasure and masturbation is really important because this is how you discover your sexual response. This will also help you develop your sexual identity and who you are. A lot of people harbour inhibitions about pleasuring themselves, and this can stem from childhood and what parents have said about touching yourself. We always think of teenage boys and masturbation and it can be associated with them. DUMP THOSE MYTHS NOW. Masturbation is for everybody. Remember you are entitled to have pleasure!

'Some people even enjoy setting the mood to enhance their experience, and light candles or have a bath; it is almost like being with a lover. Other people can just crack one off. You have to do what works for you. And then you will feel free to learn about your orgasmic response.

'The great thing about self-pleasure is that you learn the pressure, the friction, the speed, and what you like, and whether you use just fingertips or a vibrator. Some women prefer to use things like a pillow to rub against. ALL THESE THINGS ARE GOOD, because you discover how your body works. And when you do meet a new sexual partner, you can share that knowledge.'

Female pleasure and how we talk about it is, THANK GOD, rapidly changing and being championed. Celebrities are now even releasing their own sex toys. I admit I have bought both Lily Allen's fabulous clit sucking Womanizer and Gwyneth Paltrow's Goop double-ended vibrator, obviously solely on their recommendations alone. Both are excellent, by the way. Is it any surprise that both these women are divorced, happy and into self-pleasure? Across social media, women are now openly and unashamedly talking about masturbation and pleasure and taking the shame out of what was very much a male-centric wanking world.

Natalie Lee, who runs the Instagram account @stylemesunday, has been a huge advocate for exploring female pleasure, and was filmed having an orgasm for the Channel 5 programme, *How to Have a Better Orgasm*. Natalie frequently posts about the joys and benefits of wanking, as well as opening up discussions on female pleasure.

I asked Natalie why she has become such a champion for self-love. She explained that 'there are so many benefits to masturbation. Helping you get to sleep, improving your self-confidence, helping you with menstrual pain, helping you with any sort of pain, actually, and endorphins . . . There are so many benefits . . .'

Natalie is very open about getting everyone into it. She says, 'it's just about encouraging women to gain that control of their sexual desire, control of their sexual needs. I think just getting that back again is really important. It's quite revolutionary to not need somebody else to satisfy your sexual appetite. It's nice to want somebody but not need them in that kind of way, so I'm definitely all about encouraging women to gain that, and I talk about it frequently with my daughters too. We talk about exploring yourself and I feel I really missed out about masturbation and self-pleasure when I was younger. I definitely had a lot of shame around it. I didn't explore it enough and I feel like my whole sexual coming out was taken away from me because I felt like I was discovered through the hands of somebody else rather than discovering myself through myself, if that makes sense. So it's a big interest of mine and I just basically want to get the whole of the female country wanking.'

Natalie has certainly influenced me! Through my own exploration, and following accounts like Natalie's and others, in a short space of time, my perception of self-pleasure has completely changed. Rather than seeing it as something to be embarrassed about, or something that takes you away from sex with a partner, or was just unnecessary, I have begun to see it as important as exercise, meditation and drinking two litres of water a day, as well as enhancing my happiness, confidence and well-being. In fact, my new mantra is: Hydrate, Meditate, Masturbate. Not that I'm saying you have to get divorced or become single to do this or to feel this way, but it was definitely the catalyst for a significant change in my own sexual awakening journey.

My sexual confidence was something that was deeply intertwined with my own self-worth, attitudes towards my body and identifying myself as a mother, not as a separate sexual being. It is not that I didn't enjoy it; it's just that I wasn't adventurous and I realise now that I was almost fearful of it. So much so, I hadn't even looked at my own fanny until recently; I'd almost forgotten it was there. My sex drive became non-existent after the births of both my children and I now realise that I was repressed and coy about it. I would blush when I talked about sex (thanks, Mum) and there are many episodes on *The Scummy Mummies Podcast* where my sexual naivety was very much the butt of the joke (pun . . . oh, never mind).

But something very strange happened to me just weeks after my husband left; it was like my body woke up and I suddenly really wanted sex! I couldn't stop thinking about it. It was like a switch had been flicked on in my brain and I just *really* wanted to fuck all the time and to be fucked. My sex drive went from neutral to fifth gear in three weeks, and it was the most strange, confronting and confusing feeling.

And I know I am not alone in this. When I started talking to other single women about it, they confessed that they felt the same, that they too had had a sexual reawakening after a separation. Comedian Samantha Baines called it her 'sexual explosion', and that is exactly what it felt like. It still feels like this carefully guarded secret, that us older separated women only talk about in whispers. This is mainly because most of our friends are coupled up, and, to be honest, it's hard to explain to them that we are suddenly on heat. More broadly, as women in our forties and older, we have been conditioned to think it is dirty and slutty to feel like this, that it is something we should be ashamed of. But, take it from me, it's really bloody exciting and it should be celebrated.

One of the leading voices on sex in the UK is Dr Karen Gurney, aka @thesexdoctor, clinical psychologist and psychosexologist, and author of *Mind The Gap: The truth about desire and how to futureproof your sex life*. She has been working with couples for nearly two decades, so I decided to talk to her in an attempt to understand my new-found sexuality.

I asked her whether she thought there was shame in enjoying sex as an older woman.

She explained that, 'women's sexuality is shamed, full stop. The idea that women shouldn't talk it about too much is still very much part of our collective psyche, even though politically nobody agrees with it. But there's also the idea that we are all ageing and that every year people think less of us sexually; this is something that women have to deal with more than men. Women's sexual currency is very much about youth, whereas men have this whole "silver fox" thing, and as they get older their sexual currency is valued more. This is also down to the idea that the older we get, the less we should be talking about sex, and, when it comes to women, you shouldn't be having it and enjoying it. As women you are devalued the older you get.

'There's a lot of research about how women's sexual confidence and assertiveness grows as they age, and their body confidence grows too. When starting new relationships after divorce, it provides a new opportunity to show this side of yourself. We can get so typecast in our marriage about what is sex and how it looks and how a person sees you sexually, you can almost have your sexuality erased by someone else not seeing it, not valuing it, and not prioritising it. In long-term relationships, your confidence might be growing in other ways, but also taking a battering, if you don't feel desired. In a new relationship, you are not typecast, and you can be free to explore that new-found confidence.'

Getting your sexual confidence back after separating or, in fact, when you're still in a long-term relationship, is difficult, but it doesn't have to be that way. I spoke with Cherry Healey, who is one of the three women behind The Hotbed Collective, and asked about her experience of being sexually confident in the bedroom.

Cherry and I spoke about the importance of owning your pleasure and feeling comfortable using sex toys with a partner. She said, 'I'm really open-minded and I just don't worry. Nothing freaks me out, to be honest with you, but I have been with a couple of people where I've brought sex toys out and there's a bit of, "why do you need that?" And, look, I try and be gentle, because everyone's at different stages, but I think if that person isn't pretty down with it, by the third time you're with them, if that awkwardness is still there, then that's a problem for me, because I think, "You need to grow up a bit and realise that women function in a different way, women take a lot longer, or you might not be very good." But it's never that for me; it's that you could be with the best person in the world, it feels really great, but sometimes different parts of me want different stimulation. I think there is a thing for guys, where they think – Am I not enough? – which I think sometimes is true, but often it's just like, "No, but I like it."'

This new sexual confidence that Dr Gurney and The Hotbed Collective were talking about and championing, of course, for me, arrived at completely the wrong time, because the universe decided to give me the gift of a towering libido at the same time as the lockdown. For the first few months there was no chance of going out on a date, or even having a cheeky snog in a pub (or going to a pub). But I also think this is *exactly* what I needed, as I am sure in my wobbly, fragile and vulnerable state, I would have made some really unwise choices. However, I cannily saved them up, for the summer of shagging that was to come (cum).

While I couldn't physically date, I started to feel more attractive and even visible again. I remember walking down the street and I saw a handsome-ish man sitting in his car, and I spontaneously decided to make eye contact and smile at him, and then, he actually smiled back at me. Jesus Christ, I swear this first flutter of pretty lame flirting nearly blew my actual nipples off.

I mean, I had *dreams* about having sex with other people, like Ed Miliband and Ed Balls (who doesn't?), but I now realise I never really properly flirted much at all while I was married, and I didn't even know if I was any good at it. So apart from my Labour Party fantasies, I was a good wife. I had turned that part of me off, as it was a skill I thought I would never need again. Now, suddenly, it was very much back on.

'Oh my God, I can now have sex with *anyone* I want!' I thought to myself one morning, when I was emptying the lint from the tumble dryer. Then it hit me: that that would also require me getting naked in front of a whole new human being. It had been two decades since I had been intimate with anyone else, and I had only slept with a couple of people in total my whole life. So being in the nude in front of someone else was a pretty scary prospect. And especially after two pregnancies, my body was more of a sensible people mover, rather than a slick sexy Lamborghini. Not to mention that so much had changed in the dating world (and the pubic hair landscape). So the whole thing felt incredibly daunting.

Obviously all these hang-ups are entirely the patriarchy's fault and all that porn that seems so popular these days. Sex and desirability in the media has a particular look. We only have to look at popular TV programmes such as *Love Island* to be shown what is deemed 'sexy'. Skinny bodies, flawless tanned skin, absolutely zero body hair and perfectly perky boobs are all the go-to when it comes to 'sexiness'. And, worse, the actual act of sex is portrayed unrealistically, with ridiculous moaning, robotic reactions and, at times, sadly abusive undertones. There is absolutely no chance of a fanny fart or an accidental head butt included in porn. However, this Barbie Doll and Action Man imagery *does not* translate to real life and, as I discovered, sex is not a carefully choreographed performance. As a good friend once said to me, 'Jesus, Helen, don't worry about what you look like. Men will fuck anything, even a hole in the road.' I think I'm going to get this printed on a mug.

I want to shout this at everyone: you don't need to look like Kim Kardashian to get some bedroom action (or some kitchen action for that matter). As I have found out, it doesn't matter if your boobs are a bit saggy, you've got a few stray chin hairs and that your thighs do not, or will not ever, possess 'the gap', but it goes beyond not caring about what you look like and it is also about not accepting any shit or bad behaviours.

I spoke with Leyla Hussein, OBE, the Somali-born British psychotherapist and social activist, who has been a huge champion for women's rights and female pleasure. Leyla said, 'Dating is still something I'm learning about, I'm forty now and I call it the "I Don't Give a Shit" stage. I don't tolerate any shit; I don't have time to entertain that bullshit. I've also accepted that I may never get married or be in a long-term relationship with someone, but I'm learning to really enjoy myself, even if it's a three-month courtship with this person. I care more about the experience now than the length of something. I'd rather talk about the lovers I've had than the miserable relationships that I've been stuck in, and that's a shift and that shift is really good. This is why I love this stage of my life, because I can tell a guy exactly what I want, I don't have to do the whole, "of course I like football too". I mean, remember when you pretended to like their activities?

'And I love the fact I can be clear about this now and one thing I've been especially clear about is that I like two days to myself. I need that bed to myself for two days. I don't need you humping me every day – let's negotiate sex time, three times a week, four times, great, because you know what, I don't wanna get urinary infections every two weeks . . . nobody talks about that, they forget to mention that when you're having sex every day. And I'm aware of that now, I don't want to keep going to my GP. So let's negotiate and I will be the best partner you'll ever have. And they look at me like I'm crazy, like, "Oh, you don't want to live with a man?" And I'm like, no, unless you live in a mansion and have two separate sections in the house, then no, I mean I don't want to share a bathroom with a guy (again); I don't know why.'

I thought, I know why – beard hair and nail clippings.

Getting to this point of empowerment does take time. Realistically, having shared our body with only one person for years, it is perfectly normal that many of us will feel freaking terrified at flashing our bush or even our balls at someone new. These negative feelings and fears are completely understandable and it can also take time to get your confidence and your mojo back. Some people wait two weeks, two months or even years to get into sex and dating again, or they just decide that they are happier without a partner – for a bit, or at all. And all of those are OK; it is of course a very unique and individual choice, and it is a choice. You get to choose.

Dr Pam Spurr explained that, to get your mojo back, 'the starting point is always general confidence. Because it's all interlinked, if you start working on your general confidence that will translate to bedroom confidence. The first step is to listen to your inner monologue; what is that inner voice telling you? Is it telling you, "No one is going to want me," "I have let myself go," "I have nothing to offer," "Oh, look at me: I have two kids and no income; who wants this?"'

'That monologue will always have undertones that relate to your worthiness to date and eventually bed. You have to first look at that inner monologue and listen to it. And hear yourself, and what you are thinking you are. If you're always thinking, "no one is going to want me" and "OMG, I feel so worthless", you become that, because it affects how you relate to people.'

'It affects your body language. It affects your entire persona. Listen to it – it is usually an awakening for people about just how negative it is – and then start to ease up on it. Start to make changes, start to massage it into something different.'

'When you catch wind of yourself being really negative, you can say, "No, hang on a minute, I WILL meet someone." And when it comes to sex, you might be thinking, yes, I have had the same sexual routine for fifteen years. And you can feel you are never going to be good at sex, and wondering how you will relate to a new person in bed. And then you change that. You say to yourself, "This is going to be interesting, it is going to be a positive thing." You just start working on that inner voice across the board, with your general confidence and specifically your worthiness to date again and to meet a partner, and potentially a sexual partner – whatever you are looking for.'

'The next step is to set little goals. Goals that inspire you to develop that bigger broader confidence. For example, if every night you are having wine and watching Netflix, then take one night out a week to develop a new skill or hobby for yourself. Something to take you out of yourself and where you have been. It is good to show yourself you can do new things.'

'Stop focusing on what you're missing from your previous relationship and instead start focusing on what you missed out on. Ask yourself, "What did my ex stop me from doing?" Start building these things back into your life. These are the things that will build confidence as a single person.'

'When you are ready to get back out there, immersing yourself in this new world is a huge thing. There are many ways to meet a new partner, or even just to find a fuck buddy – obviously you can do this through friends or going out, but, for most people, online dating is the way in which they connect with somebody new.'

Despite not being able to physically meet a man, I jumped straight onto Tinder just a few weeks after my separation. It was part curiosity, part revenge, part new-found horniness and part insanity. Even though I have heard people talking about Tinder for years, I was not prepared for the ride I was about to take. I remember sitting up late one night and just thinking, 'Fuck him, I am now a free woman, I am going to see what's out there. I'm going to see who will want me and, more importantly, who or what I want.'

I uploaded a few photos and threw together a few sentences about myself. I remember trembling as I typed, nervous talking about myself in this way and what this actually symbolised and could lead to. I had chosen a life partner when I was nineteen years old, barely an adult and just starting to form my identity. What I looked for in a man back then was someone to build a future with, to grow up and experience all those 'firsts' with, someone who would add something to my life that I didn't think I had. Now I was different; everything was different. I had grown up, and I had two children, a house, a career and money of my own. What I really wanted now (right now) was someone to lust after and desire, and for them to desire me right back.

My profile read 'Fun, confident, loves a wine and a laugh. Left wing. Brings the party. Loves good food and running. Positive, sunny and easy-going.' That ought to do it, I thought. I neglected to include, 'was recently spectacularly dumped by my long-term partner, I am currently living off cigarettes, cheap alcohol and adrenaline and in a spectacularly vulnerable and fragile state.' But, hey, it is always good to leave a few little mysteries for people to discover.

I closed the app and didn't check it for a few days as I really needed to concentrate on going back to my break-up trauma. When I did click on the little red button, I was utterly shocked to find that not just one or two people had swiped right, but over 2,000. HOLY FUCKING SHIT! I mean, let's get things clear, most of these guys were not anything to write home about and many of them looked like they would probably chop you up and put you in the boot of their car, but a few were completely intriguing and dare I say it, delicious, or appeared to be, on first swipe. In two days, I had amassed potentially thousands of men I could have sex with, that wanted to have sex with me; what a weird planet to suddenly land on.

While I was unnecessarily giddy, flattered and excited, what also struck home was how easy it was to find sex or at least to be able to fuck a stranger. A couple of clicks and a few messages exchanged was all it would take. Having existed in the protected bubble of my little family unit, being wife and mother, and my social life revolving around my girlfriends, this felt like I was entering a parallel universe. A sex universe filled with dick pics and a shitload of new acronyms to discover and use.

I swiped and began chatting to a couple of men. While I was sexually naive, I knew within a few text exchanges what these blokes were like, and what they wanted. What was surprising was just how quickly things would get sexual. I might start the chat with, 'Hey, how you are you tonight?', and some of them would get straight in there with, 'I'm horny AF, right now!' So that was the small talk OVER WITH THEN. There was no mention or exchange of star signs or favourite Deliveroo eateries available here.

Tinder is a bear pit. You really need to search long and hard to find the gems and, be warned, there are some absolute creeps out there and you can easily find yourself in abusive situations or feel pressured to do or send things you are not comfortable with. One of the most powerful social media accounts calling out the terrible behaviour of online dating is @lalalaletmeexplain. Run by a sex, dating and relationships educator, it highlights and exposes the unacceptable behaviours both online and in person. I found the stories and confessions of online dating confronting and upsetting, but also incredibly important in terms of what I needed to look out for, and how I could protect myself, as well as explore this new experience safely.

I also signed up to Bumble, which is meant to be more female led, as the women have to make the first move. Once you get chatting, you can send pictures, and this is when I got my first REAL LIFE dick pic! OH DEAR GOD. The said photo arrived shortly into the conversation I was having with a fun and cheeky 35-year-old. He said he had just popped out of the shower and was feeling horny, so he just took a photo of his willy and sent it on through. Just like that. Having not even watched porn for over twenty years, I need to explain that I hadn't seen an erect penis for a VERY LONG TIME. And sexting and dirty talk was a language I knew nothing about, so I kicked into mum mode and replied,

'Oh, that looks fun! Well done, you!'

I obviously needed to brush up my verbal foreplay.

After spending a few weeks texting a couple of men, I started to get fond of one fellow, who was also a single parent. We would text each other and he was into the same comedy and music that I was. He was gentle, sweet and we made each other laugh. Then things escalated into something sexier and more intense. There were nights of sexting, sharing fantasies and some phone sex. In the time of Covid, these were my only opportunities for intimacy (safely), so we got creative! I quickly tapped into this new ridiculous vocabulary of words and emojis. Aubergine anyone? I felt desired, noticed and awakened to this new world. While we never met IRL (In Real Life), it was a brilliant way to kick off the beginning of this new adventure. I just had to get out there NOW and have that first post-break-up SHAG!

As the lockdown lifted and the world got slightly less restricted and scary, it was time to try dating, FOR REALZ. By this time, I was more than ready. I had got really good at getting off alone and I wanted to try out my new skills! I wanted to know what my body was going to feel like next to another human being. What they MIGHT do to me and me to them. Showtime!

One of the best things I did to prepare myself for the big event was set up a Tinder Support Group on WhatsApp. I had a couple of trusted single mum friends who were a couple of years ahead of me in the dating world and I would send them pics of the men I was considering hooking up with. This would help me decide the right way forward and, most importantly, if it was time to stop texting someone. They patiently told me everything they had learnt doing online dating and passed it on, so here's their advice with some of the knowledge I have gained too.

A Little Bit of Advice for Getting Back into Dating

- **Choose an App that Suits You** – Have a look at a few different apps and find that one that suits your personality with features that you like. I signed up to three, Tinder, Hinge and Bumble, and in the end found my favourite men on Tinder, though BE WARNED, it is essentially sex Deliveroo.

- **Use recent photos and get a friend to check your profile** – Choose a couple of pics that look like you (NO BRAINER). Then when you write your profile, get a best mate to read over it, too. Or, even better still, get a friend to write it for you.

- **Good Banter and Texting is Key** – If you feel like you have a good connection with the person via the apps or texting, then this is a good sign. It's no guarantee, but you can quickly weed out people who are going to be hard work in real life; good sex and good chat often go hand in hand.

- **Fact Check Them** – Make sure the person you meet is really who they say they are. Obviously if they are on social media, or tell you their full name, you can do a quick google, and that is a good way to check if they are real. A quick FaceTime chat can solve this problem too. Then you'll know if those photos are recent or not.

- **Send Raunchy Pics Safely** – If you are going to send sexy photos to each other, don't include pictures of your face.

Photos can be easily shared and you do not know who they will share it with.

- **Be Clear About What You Want** – If you are going to meet up and have sex, don't be shy about asking for what you want or what you do and don't like. And make sure they know you that you ALWAYS USE PROTECTION. If you are straight, it is surprising how many men don't want to use it, or just expect you to take control of this, so set your rules out before you meet.

- **Don't Do the Chasing** – If it is always you initiating the conversations then hold back and wait for them to text or call you. It shouldn't feel one-sided or that you are the one that has to be organising everything. You're not their mothers.

- **Back-up Crew** – Let one or two friends know you are meeting someone new and where you're meeting them. You can tell them who this person is if you want to as well. Also, if you want an excuse to leave an awkward date, get them to call you with a fake emergency.

- **You Owe Them Nothing** – If at any point you don't feel comfortable on text or in person, end things. Hang up. Block them. Or leave the date or their house. You can be polite by all means, but don't feel you have to give the other person anything you don't want to. EVER.

- **Meet in a Neutral Place** – It is good to have the initial meeting somewhere like a pub, or bar, or even just go for a walk in a park. Don't commit to a dinner. You will know whether it is worth meeting again, or whether you want to get home as quickly as possible and get down to it.

- **Don't Get Too Pissed** – A few warm-up drinks are perfectly good for relaxing things, but sometimes that sixth cocktail doesn't help you make the best choices. Also, when you're pissed, it is much harder to orgasm.

- **You Don't Need a Bald Fanny** – Hairy or smooth, have a hairstyle down there that makes you happy, not what you think your partner wants you to have. Have a full Hollywood if that makes you happy or go with a full seventies bush.

- **Wear Something You Love** – This is the same as the rule for body hair. Wear what makes you feel confident and sexy. Also, if you think there is a chance of a shag, take a few things with you, like spare knickers, even a sneaky toothbrush, face wipes and deodorant. Or whatever makes you feel good. If you have to take a cab or train ride home, it is nice to feel a little bit human afterwards.

- **Be Your Own Pleasure Boss** – Know what you like before you take it to the next level. And don't be shy about asking for what makes YOU feel good. Most partners are turned on by a confident lover and if something is hurting or doesn't feel good, just say so. And have fun.

- **Sex is Awkward and Funny** – Porn tells lies, people. It isn't all soft lighting, silk sheets and sultry moaning. It is two (or sometimes three) bodies just going for it. Chances are there is going to be the occasional funny noise or awkward bit when you're changing positions. It is OK to have a laugh and be playful and silly.

- **Sex Toys Add to the Fun** – If you have a favourite vibrator or dildo, that can be involved in the activities too. Just experiment and enjoy what gives you the best time.

- **Make your own Rules** – Look, we are all grown-ups now. You know what you like and want and need. You are having sex as an adult, not a teenager; you know how to stay safe, and you don't need me to tell you what to do. Just go on, get out there, try stuff, and have a brilliant shag. You'll thank me for it.

Get me, telling you all what to do, after having only dated for a year. So, have I always followed this advice? NO, I HAVE NOT, because, as much as I *know* the right things to do, there were times when there was a thrill in not behaving as I *should*. I wasn't always safe and I wasn't always sober. But it was all part of my process and, as my friend and psychologist Dr Rachel Master wisely told me, 'being newly divorced is very much like a second adolescence, and as such we are compelled to rebel, break rules and make some mistakes.'

As much as I wanted to feel free and rebellious, STIs are not something to take lightly. Dr Karen adds, 'There's a huge rise in STIs in women who are coming out of long-term relationships. Newly single women in their forties and fifties is where we see a lot of new STIs in my work in sexual health. Particularly women who are on contraception or are post-menopausal, because they're women who are not used to having sex with a condom. We are seeing a big rise in STIs in that age range and this is something that is showing in research as well. When you are newly single, it is a bit of a vulnerable time for sexual health; I am aware of that. It is something that can really affect women's confidence if they are then tested positive for herpes or HIV, as it's not something that they ever expected. All STIs are manageable, even if they are lifelong. But if you are newly single and just getting over a divorce, then this is not what you need. It also affects women's future confidence about how desirable they will be in the future to new partners. It is really important to have that confidence to talk about what you want and about using condoms. Being assertive about what you want is important and saying using a condom is non-negotiable. But I understand you have to have a certain underlying confidence to get to that level.'

The first time I actually popped my first post-divorce cherry was with a mix of excitement, hilarity and a challenge to my feminist principles. I had met an Aussie guy on Bumble. I followed some of the rules, I chatted to him on the phone and had some good funny conversations. He sent me a few dick pics and made an extensive list of what he was intending to do to me and promised me a lot of orgasms. And then he said he would drive over to my place and cook me dinner and bring me some nice wine. 'That sounds lovely!' I replied, and then I realised that I had just agreed to let a complete stranger into my house. BUT it was a great excuse to clean my house and use the candelabra that had been sitting on the piano getting dusty.

He came over on a Saturday night, cooked me a steak dinner in my kitchen, and we drank a couple of bottles of fancy red. Quickly after that, we started kissing and took off our clothes. As I was thinking things were getting close to the action, I brought the condoms out. 'Oh, I don't want to use those things,' he said. And I simply replied, 'Well, we're not going to have sex unless you put it on, so it's up to you.' Not surprisingly, standing there with a full erection, he decided that perhaps having safe sex was a good option! And once we had popped on the johnny, we had a good old-fashioned bonk! The positives that I took from this first time was how my size 18, stretch-marked, wobbly, hairy, imperfect body was not an issue at all. Having stressed over it, and made a list of all faults before he arrived, once we got kissing, it did not fucking matter. In fact, he kept saying things like, 'Oh my God, you're so sexy!', and 'You're so beautiful, Helen.' And look, I know people say all sorts of shit in the moment, but this was extraordinary to me. He was right: I did feel sexy. I *am* sexy.

He then decided to stay over and proceeded to SNORE ALL NIGHT. And I couldn't sleep, because I was giddy as a teenager, so I stayed awake all night, listening to him sound like a tractor, and texting my Aussie mates things like,

'OMG, I just had sex!'

In the morning, we had sex again, and during it his phone rang. I thought, surely he's not going to answer it, but he *did*. I was on my back with him actually in me and then he suddenly was leaning over and picking up his phone and saying in a broad Australian accent, 'MAAAATTTTE, how's it going?'

I got up, made myself some coffee and put together some smoked salmon bagels for us both. He eventually stopped talking and as he got ready to leave, he seemed keen to see me again, and I said, 'Sure, it would be great to see you again' – knowing full well I probably wouldn't. But it was done. I had done it. And now I was ready for more!

OK, let's stop a minute; what did I learn from this? What behaviours did I just exhibit here? What are the big red flags that are waving in my face? Answering the phone and being inside a vagina at the same time is not OK. Me making him breakfast and acting like a hotel housemaid is NOT OK. Accepting bad behaviour and acting like you did in your marriage is not fucking OK.

The first time you have sex after a break-up is inevitably a bit shambolic, but, for many of us, we just want to GET IT DONE. Samantha Baines told me about her first encounter. She said, 'I was chatted up the first time I left the house, which was kind of incredible, because my opinion of myself being sexy was so low, so to have that early on was ... I almost thought I was being punk'd, because it was the first time literally I'd been out. I thought, has like my sister paid someone to chat me up, so I feel better? So he chatted me up and then we organised a date a week later and we had sex, and it was weird, because he ordered pizza and then three pizzas came and we had to stop having sex, for the pizzas. And he was like, "Do you want some pizza?" And I said, "No, it's one in the morning." And then he sat there and ate pizza and we were just naked in his bed and his room was really messy ... At the time I was just so grateful that someone found me attractive and that he desperately wanted to have sex with me, and so I was like, "This is great!" Whereas now I'd be more like, "How dare you pick pizza over my vagina!"'

After my clunky sexual start, it was time to see if I could do better next time. I got back on Tinder and found a wonderfully interesting and handsome artist and he reawakened a side of me I had buried for a long time. I had spent fifteen years working in and studying contemporary art, before I started comedy full time, and it felt exciting to feel smart and interesting and be with someone creative and so wildly different from my ex.

We stayed up late and talked for hours about his life growing up in Ghana and making art in New York and London – there wasn't even a hint of sexy time. But then it got to 2am and we were both getting tired, and he leaned in and kissed me. And then it went all frantic and handsy. He was kind, funny and gloriously enthusiastic. We ended up staying up most of the night, just talking and fucking, and then I fell asleep in his arms as he stroked my hair and held me. It was a tenderness I hadn't felt for what felt like forever.

We saw each other every Friday night for six weeks after that. I thought, what a brilliant arrangement: I get to spend the week with my kids, and do my work, and see friends in the park, and once a week a nice man pops over for art chats, drinks and sex, and goes home. I felt empowered by this set-up. However, as much as I adored his creativity, he was also creative when it came to making plans and texting me back. And one night, when he said he was going to turn up, his phone was turned off, and he didn't show. His excuse was that his phone had died. That feeling of rejection and abandonment really stung; I was still vulnerable and dealing with the trauma of the separation, and this rattled me.

I did what most sensible people do and drank about two bottles of wine, had a cry and then woke up on my bed, naked, lying face down like a starfish at 5am, feeling sad and rough. I called him up and broke things off between us. And while I felt upset, as cheesy as it sounds, I was proud of myself. I wasn't accepting bad behaviour and it felt GOOD. Sure, I really liked him, but I liked myself more.

Strangely enough, the artist and I remained really good friends. Asserting myself, and putting myself first, and telling him what I didn't like, didn't make him run away; in fact, it established boundaries that we both obviously needed.

So, did I keep looking on dating apps for more sex? Oh, of course I did.

This was when I decided that future interactions with men were going to be an opportunity for me to start observing how I behaved around them, learning how to continue to develop my own self-worth and how I chose to take ownership of the situation. This new phase of my life was about my own sexual evolution and revolution. The most significant realisation for me was that I do not need a man for anything other than sex (and maybe flirting). I liked sex and wanted pleasure, but, apart from that, I had everything else I could possibly want right now and that felt pretty good.

Clementine Ford told me, 'It has been so liberating dating now that I have had a child; I can connect with that side of myself without thinking is this man is going to be the most important person in my life. The most important person in my life is my kid, and after that it's my friends, and they might be able to join the friends in some capacity, but they will never be able to walk into my house and kick off their shoes in the middle of the floor and leave them there; that is just never going to happen.'

This is just how I felt too. This massive shift in my needs and self-worth was one of the biggest contributing factors to getting happy.

Dr Karen Gurney explains that, 'There is something unique about women who are separated now, who are financially secure. In your twenties and early thirties, marriage and kids bring a certain security, a lifestyle security, but they also bring a massive burden of housework and childcare. The women I work with who become single in their forties, fifties, sixties and seventies, say "why would I want anything apart from the sex? Because what I know is that I will end up doing all the washing, cleaning and cooking." And I know a lot of women who will say, "I never want to live with a man again. I don't want anything regular. I don't need that, and all I will get from that is grief." But men are different. Men are desperate for that; they need that friendship and intimacy. However, women can get that from other women, and don't need that from a man. Men are used to someone looking after them, even in the most feminist of relationships.

'Divorced women are in a powerful position, especially if they have their own career and money and house and are not anxious about their financial situation, because, for the first time in their dating life, they are not looking for commitment.

'For those of us who settled down in our late teens and early twenties, the criteria for choosing someone might not have been sex as the number one priority. It might have been in the top five, but you might have been looking for someone who you could have kids with, or a laugh with, or go on holiday with, and then that changed when you got older. You now discover you are choosing someone based on attraction and sexual compatibility. It doesn't matter if you don't like their mates or they don't earn much money, which might have mattered when you were much younger.'

When the summer came along I was very much up for exploring my new-found confidence. I had a few weeks alone, and decided to rethink who I was going to try to meet. On the dating apps, I had set my age range from 28 to 48 years, as a 41-year-old woman, thinking why the fuck not? There seemed to be a couple of cute young men who had swiped me, which I thought was a little odd, thinking, Oh, they must have made a mistake, I don't deserve someone that young and hot.

Why did I do that? Why did I put myself down, when we all know older men have absolutely no problems dating gorgeous younger women? And, as a feminist, I think it is my God-given right and duty to reverse this.

So, one afternoon I replied to an extremely handsome thirty-one-year-old chap. I told him I was curvy, forty-one and Australian, and he said he was into older women. It was also very convenient as I was doing a gig at the Clapham Grand that night, and he just happened to live in Clapham.

I texted him at 6pm, met him at the pub at 9.30pm, we chatted, had a few drinks, a fantastic snog in the street and then back to my place in a taxi at 11pm. The next few hours were incredible. I won't go into details, but suffice to say I am pretty sure he rearranged my internal organs with his impressive manhood and did all sorts of brilliant MAGICAL things with his hands. He was very much into making sure I was having a good time. It was safe, consensual and thrilling. And there was very much an understanding it was just a one-off for us both.

We sat in bed together afterwards and chatted about what dating was like for us, him as a young man, and me as an older woman. I showed him what men looked like on Tinder, and how none of the older blokes can take a proper selfie. He told me about young and older women and what his rules were. The one thing I remember him saying was: 'if they don't show a picture of themselves smiling, then they have bad teeth.' Remember this one, people.

It was like a cultural exchange, refreshing and honest. He asked me what my Instagram handle was, and I felt about 25 years old, and when he saw that I had 140,000 followers and an official 'blue tick' account, he clapped and said, 'OMG, I fucked someone who is verified!' Then we had a cuddle, and he hopped in a taxi to Clapham. We both got what we wanted, and I got to go back to sleep.

While I laughed about the fact my lover was impressed by my public profile, it did make me begin to worry how much my potential dates could find out about me before they even met me, or, even worse still, what they knew about me that they could share.

It made me wonder, how do you date when you have a large following and are known widely for professional reasons? Or more specifically, for me, how difficult does this make getting those cheeky one-night stands?

Leyla Hussein told me, 'I mean it's still tough, now I have the layer of having this public profile. I mean, now online dating's tricky. I have to change my name, or they're like, "Are you Leyla Hussein, the one who tried to chase Theresa May with a vagina costume!" and I'm like, "Yes, that's me, how are you?" So I've now reached that stage with dating where I'm getting my friends to set me up, out of safety, and I think because of the work that I do, you know, talking about the patriarchy and female sexuality and the control of women's bodies, they think I'm running a dungeon. I mean, some men interpret this – me talking about sex all the time and women's pleasure – like that, and I'm like, "Dude, I'm talking about it all the time because I don't have time to get any. I'm using my panels to talk about this." So there's this assumption where men are targeting me for that reason and they're quite shocked when I'm crocheting and drinking tea, so dating is quite tricky, especially when you live with a little bit of a profile. And then there are the African men, who want their potential submissive wife, or the white guys who see me as some sort of fetish, so it's really hard to date out there. You have to scan people. I have to call my security team, and seriously for security reasons. I mean, I have got a few fatwas on me, so I don't know, I mean my potential date could kill me – like really, it's a thing.'

While I didn't have any fatwa on me, speaking to Leyla was a good kick up the arse in terms of how careful I had to be, but I was determined to feel empowered by my new love of sex and the control I was feeling.

I told a few friends about what I had got up to with this hot young thing. Most of them were happy for me and were relieved I was still alive after meeting a stranger, but a few of them said things to me like, 'Oh Helen, you are fucking around like a man!' I'm sure it was *meant* to be a compliment, but does fucking around 'like a man' mean enjoying sex with whoever you like? Because I think women do that, too. And more of us women are doing it. It's fascinating, in this day and age, the language we use to describe women who like sex.

As Dr Karen revealed, 'some of the data around women dating younger men, the whole "cougar" rhetoric, is that it is the perfect mix of the balance of power. Older women feel more powerful and sexually confident when they have sex with younger men. They don't need anything from the young lovers other than to have sex. And also the younger men value that relationship and that makes women feel great, too. But people aren't really talking about this, and married people are also jealous of this.'

After that encounter with the young man, I was buoyed by the experience and keen to meet new and interesting people. I had the two nights a week to myself, and I referred to that as my 'sex window'. For the other five nights, I was Mum and that was incredibly important. I focused on my children, who, like me, were getting used to a new way of living. But, on the weekend, I could be fulfilled in other ways. There were times I would go on dates and it would be clear that there wasn't anything there between us; we'd have a couple of drinks, and politely part ways. As my sister kept telling me, 'Helen, you don't have to give every man your vagina!' And that was true. But when it was good, safe and exciting, I got to do that too (if I wanted).

Over a few months, I met and slept with some fabulously interesting and sexy men including a hunky and charming six foot four French man, a saucy posh photographer (who had a penis like a Pringle tube) and romantic Portuguese pastry chef who would send videos of him playing me songs on his guitar. Some of them I met a few times, others were just tantalising one-offs and some I have become friends with. Funny old Tinder. Who knew?

There was one stand-out man. He had a daughter the same age as mine, so we shared parenting stories and he seemed perfect. He made my brain sparkle and my body fizz. We made each other laugh with our filthy senses of humour, and he was kind. And the sex . . . I have never had anything like it. We met once and then he had to go to Europe for the summer holidays. We spent endless hours and days texting, and then, three weeks later, I didn't hear from him one night . . . He'd met up with an old girlfriend and, well, decided to start things up again. He sent me the most heartbreaking texts about how wonderful I was and how I deserved love, and how sorry he was. I cried all morning and had to spend a day in bed. It was a nice way of the universe telling me that there were some good men out there, but it wasn't the right time.

A year ago, I was shy and unadventurous, and having a monthly bit of 'in and out' was about as exciting as it got. Becoming this new sexually charged woman has been a huge and exciting step for me. I have made plenty of mistakes and got myself into many embarrassing situations; I even once accidentally sent a picture of my fanny to my neighbour (I wouldn't recommend doing that, btw). But embracing this sexual energy has significantly helped to boost my confidence, and my sense of control and power as a woman. And, as a bonus, I have discovered I am now at a professional level of wanking.

I'm still learning so much about the heady world of dating apps. It is definitely as addictive as social media, and getting those thrills from sexting and flirting are fun, but, to be honest, they aren't as important or nourishing as my friendships and all the other brilliant aspects of my life. The biggest change I have felt is that I no longer look to men to complete or validate me; I now know I am fucking fantastic and fantastic at fucking. Sure, it's great to have a magnificent shag with a 31-year-old every few weeks, but I can be just as happy having a nice night in with a box set, a kebab and Gwyneth's double ender.

Things I have learnt about pleasure, dating and sex

- Masturbation is a wonderful thing. Get into it any way you can. Use sex toys or just your fingers and hands, and learn how to make yourself feel amazing. There is no shame in making yourself orgasm, and it will make sex with a new partner even better.

- Sexy is not a dress size. Sexy is not a number. Sexy is not how much hair you have on your body, or how tiny your pants are. Sexy is how you feel.

- Take charge of your own pleasure and safety. It is so important to be honest about what you want and how you like it. You do not owe anyone anything. You can block sexting and you can walk away from sex at any point you like. You are in control.

- Before starting online dating, make sure you know what to look out for in terms of behaviours and pitfalls. It can be really exciting and fun; just approach it with a clear head and know what you want.

- Loving sex and having a libido is fucking brilliant – celebrate it. But, yes, perhaps you don't need to tell your friends absolutely every detail.

- Never send a picture of yourself naked with your face in it. Top down only, people.

- So far Portuguese lovers are the best; French, a close second.

FINAL WORDS

So, that was my story of becoming single, and the adventures and deep soul-searching I went through to become the happiest I have ever been. This whole year, to me, feels as if *Neighbours* had been written and directed by David Lynch, on acid, and set in a fire station in Kent. It has been the craziest, most frightening, confronting and yet most rewarding year of my life. Whilst it has involved so many tears, so much Chardonnay, too much awkward sexting and hours of therapy, I have been smothered in laughter, unconditional love, wise words, and numerous homemade lasagnes.

When I recount some of the wacky experiences I went through to get to this new blissful state, most people's jaws drop in disbelief. I hear things like, 'Why *did* you have a puffy fanny eye for two months?', Just how many firemen did it take to remove your wedding ring?', 'No, he didn't answer the phone when he was doing *that*, did he?'. Half the time it's hard to believe those things actually happened to me too. But they did and I have the eyepatches to prove it.

I have learnt so much about grief, anger, push-up bras and my alcoholic limits, as well as understanding just how fucking strong I am. And, most importantly, I now know that one comedy wife is worth more than a hundred husbands.

As I look forward to this new single life ahead of me, and that big divorce party I am planning, I look into my wardrobe and see two Vivienne Westwood dresses hanging in there, side by side.

One smaller, constricted, full of hooks, zips and in a size and shape that wouldn't let me breathe. And the other, curvy, stretchy, fun and sexy, and something I don't have to shrink myself to fit into. I like this new dress very much, and so does everyone I love.

The anniversary of my separation, just by chance, fell on the same day of my last divorce meeting with my ex. As we finally signed off as to who would get what, I realised that a year ago almost to the minute, I had discovered the truth about my husband. Things had spookily come full circle in exactly a year.

I never thought I was capable of getting through the things I did in the last twelve months, but I did, and so can you – in your own time, and in your own way. I know how frightening separation can seem, but you are all capable of surviving this; there is so much support out there for every step of the way, and a whole new happier world to enjoy and explore.

I do often wonder what my life would have looked like if I hadn't picked up that jacket and looked in the pocket that night. Thank God my daughter decided to change her mind at the last minute. Would I still be married; would I have still been holding on to that relationship and to him? I may now be sitting in a freshly renovated house, with an extra bedroom, a fancier kitchen, and bathroom that didn't leak, but instead I have a house that is practically falling down, half the size, but has twice as much love, joy and cats.

I adore my new life with just me, my two brilliant children and my adorable overweight fur babies. I am now free to be my true glorious self. And I am glad I went through all these insane events, because I wouldn't change anything, to feel the way I do right now.

Well, maybe I wouldn't have got into that hot tub.

ACKNOWLEDGEMENTS

I am incredibly grateful to the many people who have supported me and this book. Writing about a traumatic event, while you're living through it, isn't easy, and there were many days I sat at my computer and sobbed while reliving some of the harder moments, but also I laughed a lot at the ridiculous ones. It has been incredibly cathartic, to say the least.

Firstly, I want to say thank you to my editor Sam Jackson, who had faith I could write a funny, honest and raw book about divorce in just three months! And to all the incredible experts and comedians who contributed their stories and wisdom to this book – I am so grateful for your time and encouragement! Also thanks goes to the many wonderful women who shared their stories of strength and survival with me through Scummy Mummies.

Huge love to my wonderful family who, despite being in Australia, have supported and encouraged me to keep going, even when I was feeling broken. Thank you, Mum and Dad, for always making me feel loved, and for all those kind words. To my brilliant three brothers, John, Hugh and Henry, who are all such top blokes and would do anything for me. And my magnificent sisters-in-law, Caroline and Giselle, who are like sisters and best friends to me.

And my amazing sister Claire – my champion, my therapist, my partner-in-crime – I can't even begin to thank you for everything you have done for me. You were the one who said, your story is going to make an amazing book one day, Helen. And you were right.

Special thanks to the amazing Jane Bodie, my sister-in-law and most excellent drinking and smoking buddy. Thank you for transcribing all these fabulous interviews, and for the many late-night 'writer's corner' on Zoom, where we moulded this enormous beast of a book, and made sure I didn't sound like I was drunk when I wrote it. In a nutshell, you are just glorious.

To my gorgeous friend Sarah Ream, who whipped my words into shape, and provided me with such brilliant feedback and was there on the end of the phone when I needed it most.

To Caz for your understanding and support and for being a wonderful aunty to my children.

To my wonderful and wacky neighbours who are there for me every single day. I couldn't have survived this past year without you all circling me with kindness, wine and cakes. I love you Jo, Joy, Becky, Claire, Lisa, Alice and Shiree and the rest of the motley crew.

To my three wise women: Taryn, Ceinwen and Shannon-Kate – fuck, what a massive job you have all had, holding me together. Thank you for reading all the sections of the book, for grounding me, for laughing with me, for getting angry, for being exceptional feminists and for all the 'keep going' messages when I didn't feel like I could do this.

To my friend and 'house angel' Nicola who comes to my house every week, makes it sparkle and gossips with me over a coffee and a fag.

To all my school mum friends, especially Rose and Indi who were there for me while I homeschooled and tried to write the book. Thank you for sweeping me up in your arms and just being so bloody kind and fun.

Thank you to the absolutely fabulous Arabella Weir, who came up with the title of the book over a spectacularly boozy lunch. You are magnificent in so many ways, and always an inspiration.

To fancy Annabel and wonderful Emilie, for just being such excellent women and letting me wee on your lovely kitchen chair, I have never witnessed such heights of friendship.

To the Forest Hill crew Victoria, Jemma, Honey, Charlotte, Anna, Collette, Kate, Rose, Tory, all the Sarahs, Deborah, Heather and all the women who I have shared a bottle of fizz and a laugh with. What a joy this corner of London is.

Dr Rachel Master, I am so lucky you're in my life. Thanks for the endless dating and divorce advice and wise words. You are such an impressive woman.

To my Glorious Bitches – Cherry, Hollie, Clemmie, Emma, Cat, Gayle, Lydia, Anna, Charlotte, Natalie, Steph, Zoe, Annie and Ellie. Thank you for coming to my rescue many times. And for sending me the most beautiful gifts and treats. And to Emily and Kate who have got me through so many highs and lows and reassured me I could pull this whole book thing off.

Thank you to Fernando for being such a good friend to me when I have been writing this book, and for sharing the same filthy sense of humour. To the amazing Kojo who brought art back into my life again, and makes me smile when he dances in front of his beautiful paintings. To my favourite pastry chef Nelson, thanks for the smiles, guitar playing and Portuguese treats. And to Mr B who is utterly charming and provides the most captivating late-night chats.

To Aussie comedy legend Nelly Thomas, who has kept me grounded, and made me laugh until I wet myself. Thanks for inspiring me every day with the work that you do. Love you lots, ya Mole.

To my trainer Suzanne Keatley, who made me stronger and encouraged me to lift heavier weights! And to Suzy Shand, my Pilates teacher, who literally helped put me back together again. To Nikki Hill, who got me through that huge three-week cleanse, thanks for your warmth and encouragement, and amazing sense of humour. And to my therapist, Gill, who has incredible wisdom and compassion, and has made me emotionally and mentally stronger.

God, how do I begin to thank Ellie Gibson? Dude, you are the bravest, most brilliant, caring and strongest woman I have ever met. Thank you for being my rock through all of this shit, and for supporting me doing this big solo project, while you carried the heavy load of work for the Scummy Mummies. You never fail to impress me with your resilience, your unconditional love, and your unwavering determination. And to your wonderful family: Pete, Charlie and Joe, Jimbo and Ray and the wonderful Inga.

And, finally, to my most amazing children, Matilda and Hugo, who are my everything. I feel so lucky to have them in my life, who fill my days with endless joy, love and fish fingers. This year has not been easy, but we have had so many laughs, cuddles, film nights and Haribo. Never stop singing, telling silly jokes and dancing. You're both my shining stars and I am proud of you both every day. I love our little family of three plus the two fat cats, and all the adventures we have been on together. Can't wait to see what our future holds.

Helen Thorn is an award winning comedian, podcaster and author and one half of the mildly successful comedy duo Scummy Mummies, with Ellie Gibson. She is a single mother, and has two children and two spoilt cats, who all live together in a wonky wooden house in South East London.

Originally from a tiny town in country Australia, Helen began her career in contemporary art working for several leading art galleries and museums, both in Australia and the UK, as well at the Venice Biennale in 2003. She began her stand-up career in Melbourne in 2004 and quickly gained success as a solo performer, winning competitions, and having a regular spot on an arts and culture programme on ABC TV.

In 2006, she moved to the UK, had a couple of children and then was very tired for several years. She had all but given up comedy, but on one sleepless night in 2013, while breastfeeding, on a whim she decided to book herself a five-minute open spot at a club down the road, and at that gig she met Ellie. And that changed everything.

In July 2013, they launched *The Scummy Mummies Podcast*, which has been a huge international hit and is now listened to in over 150 countries and has had over five million downloads. They have performed their live theatre show to sold-out crowds across the UK, and, in 2019, had a sell-out run at the Edinburgh Fringe Festival.

In 2016, they released a chart-topping book, *Scummy Mummies*, and have written for and featured in the *Telegraph*, *The Sunday. Times*, the *Guardian* and the *Evening Standard*, and many more. They have appeared on Woman's Hour, BBC Radio 2, 3, 4, 5 Live and 6 Music and on ITV's *Lorraine* and *Good Morning Britain*.

Helen also runs a successful fashion account on Instagram called Helen Wears a Size 18, and, in 2019, launched *Fat Lot of Good*, a body-positive podcast. She's written and appeared on several podcasts talking about body acceptance and plus size fashion, as well as her new life as a single parent. She would really like a day off one of these days.